STUDIES

IN

JOCULAR LITERATURE.

A POPULAR SUBJECT MORE CLOSELY

CONSIDERED.

BY

W. CAREW HAZLITT.

Ne moy reproues sans cause, quar mon entent est de
bone amour.

LONDON:

ELLIOT STOCK, 62 PATERNOSTER ROW

1890

REPUBLISHED BY
GALE RESEARCH COMPANY, BOOK TOWER, DETROIT, 1969

Library of Congress Catalog Card Number   67–24352

CONTENTS.

STUDIES IN
JOCULAR LITERATURE

CHAPTER I.

INTRODUCTORY REMARKS ON THE REAL USE AND IMPORTANCE OF JESTS AND ANECDOTES.

ONE of the Anglo-Saxon kings gave the manor of Walworth to his jester Nithardus; and we have all heard how the magnificent benefaction of St. Bartholomew's Hospital, subsequently repaired by Sir Richard Whittington, was founded by Rahere, the *joculator* and favourite of a later monarch of this isle. In former days, to be a fool within certain lines, or a buffoon of a special type, was a walk of

1

life not to be despised either by a man or by his friends. The jokes which he made were negotiable securities of first-class value. Not a five-pound note, but broad lands and the smiles of a prince, awaited the fortunate utterer of the *bon-mot* and the fountain of merriment and good humour.

Even in the time of Charles II. the prosperity of the vocation had sensibly declined. Charles liked people who contributed to his amusement; but shabby constitutional restraints precluded him from endowing a pleasant fellow, who could play a conjurer's tricks with the risible muscles and the purse-strings of his sovereign, with a large and valuable estate.

Nay, before the Stuart era, Henry VII., whose parsimony has been exaggerated, and who gave freely to many charitable objects, had to content himself with presenting the makers of *jeux d'esprit* with a few shillings—the shillings, of course, of that epoch.

The greater rarity of learning, and its status as a special mystery or cult, surrounded these ancient scholars with an atmosphere which we have not only a difficulty, but a sort of delicacy, perhaps, in thoroughly penetrating, so as to enable us to arrive at an absolutely accurate valuation of their gifts. Among their contemporaries and even immediate descendants they were regarded as something more than human; and this sentiment, while it, as a rule, limited itself to worshipful awe, not unfrequently degenerated into a superstitious dread fatal to the possessors of incomprehensible faculties.

The first impression of nine persons out of ten, on taking up a Book of Jests or Anecdotes, is that it is merely a volume prepared for their momentary diversion— to be bought at a stall for a trifle, cursorily studied, and thrown on one side.

But the moment that one approaches this description of literature in a critical spirit, it begins to wear a changed, and yet perhaps a more interesting, aspect. The application of a microscope of very inconsiderable power is found by a philosophical student of the subject to be adequate to the detection of much that is new and curious, lying either on the surface or not very far from it.

Anecdote-literature, in which I always desire to understand as included the Jest, seems to me fairly resonant with the life of other days—in larger measure than has been usually supposed, simply because on a superficial view we are very apt to content ourselves with the foregone conclusion, that a story, whether humorous or otherwise, is nothing but a story.

The notes to the series of Old English Jest-Books, edited by myself in 1864, and the frequent citations of such works in our philological literature, bring us to the consideration of another point of view, in which it is well, perhaps, that we should try to tolerate these facetious miscellanies, and regard with indulgence their sins alike against propriety and against wit. A dull story is frequently redeemed, it may be observed in studying such publications, by the light which it sheds on an otherwise unintelligible phrase or allusion—or, indeed, by the service which it renders in having rescued one from oblivion.

The accidental formation, more than

twenty years ago, of this acquaintance with our own jocular literature, and the periodical renewal of it in an editorial capacity, have naturally led me to pay rather close attention to the JEST in its numerous varieties and stages of growth, and to cast from time to time a scrutinising eye over the contents of the extensive series of works in this class which has come under my notice.

The result, almost unconsciously to myself, has been that the theory on the subject, with which I started in life, has made room for one of a different complexion and drift; and I propose to offer in the following pages some suggestions for reducing to a better and more intelligent order certain of the *facetiæ* and *jeux d'esprit*, by way of sample, in the Collections, and to point out, to the best of my ability, how they have been subjected to disguising or transforming processes by political, literary, or commercial inducements.

Although the independent reading of the more thoughtful and studious had long brought them, of course, to a more enlightened inference, I almost apprehend that, until Mr. Wright's volume on Grotesque and Caricature appeared, the loose general notion was that there was not much worth regarding in the present direction beyond the imperishable pages of Joe Miller; and I certainly think that a very narrow minority conceived in how wide and many-sided a meaning the Jest is susceptible of being understood.

On the contrary, the Jest offers itself to our consideration in a surprising diversity of types and garbs; and the project which I have now before me is, in fact, an attempt to treat for the first time, in a catholic and critical spirit, a theme which has been usually viewed as frivolous and undignified.

It is a matter of notoriety that some of our best antiquaries have loved to trace to their sources the comic and romantic tales which we have borrowed from the Continent, and to note the variations introduced for the sake of novelty, local requirement, or dramatic exigency, by a succession of writers in the same or in different languages.

A vast amount of labour and scholarship has been expended in illustrating by this light the works of Shakespear and our other early playwrights, as well as in recovering the clues to the material on which Chaucer and Spenser built their undying productions. Moreover, both in England and abroad, a great deal has been achieved in elucidating the literary history of our ancient jest-books, and improving our intimacy with the true origin of the stories and their subsequent adventures, in more or less numerous disguises, from the *Hundred Merry Tales* to *Joe Miller* or what may perhaps be termed the *Milleriana*.

But when one has assiduously sifted all this learning, one finds that it very naturally limits itself, as a rule, to the very early books, so far as *facetiæ* are concerned,—to that branch of the subject which belongs to Archæology; and, in short, I do not know that I have been to any but the most trifling extent forestalled in the design which I here try to carry out, of arranging and analysing the humorous traditions which we have

received from our forefathers touching
the celebrities of all ages and countries,
yet more exclusively those who flourished
within a measurable distance of time,
or those whom no distance of time is
capable of affecting ; or, once more, such
relations as owe, not to the names, but
to the matter, their continuity of life.

The origin of all jocular or semi-serious
literature and art is referable, of course,
to a stage of human development when
the deviation from a certain standard of
feeling or opinion could be appreciable ;
and it does not require the long establishment of a settled society, judging
from the habits of savage and illiterate
communities, before a sense of the ludicrous and grotesque begins to form part
of the popular sentiment.

The ludicrous and grotesque are, to a
certain extent, relative or conditional terms.
The canons of propriety and right in
primitive life are so widely different from
those which prevail in a state of civilisation,
that what we should regard as fit material
for a jest-book is elsewhere treated as a
piece of serious history.   A departure

from the line of expression or deportment
sanctioned by common usage has proved
in all countries and all ages a fertile source
of satire and caricature; but then that line,
like the needle, is subject to variation, and
the fixture of character is not, as is the case
with straight and curved lines in mathe-
matics, a matter of doctrine and fact, but
one mainly of local circumstance and
costume.

The joke has proved in all ages a
factor of manifold power and use. It
has ridiculed and exposed corruptions in
the body politic and in the social
machinery. It has laughed at some
things because they were new, and at
others because they were old. It has
preserved records of persons and ideas,
and traits of ancient bygone manners,
which must otherwise have perished; and
it frequently stands before us with its
esoteric moral hidden not much below
its ostensible and immediate purport.

Jests present humanity to our observation in its holiday attire, its Sunday best,
or at least under some exceptional and
temporary aspect. Quin and Foote,

Mathews and Sydney Smith, Frank Talfourd and Henry Byron, had their grave, and very grave, intervals. Hood himself said that he had to be a lively Hood for a livelihood; and it was mournfully true, as the records of his every-day life, chastened by illness and sorrow, only too well establish. The pleasant or comic episodes may be an occasional incidence of the least happy existence or the least fortunate career; and the anecdotes, humorous or otherwise, of celebrated men and women are receivable with allowance as traits of character and conduct, for which some special circumstance, or a union of circumstances, is answerable. In the general tenor of the most favoured experiences the serious element is apt to preponderate; the heyday of our years is like short, intermittent sunshine; and we ought to come to the study of ANA, if we wish to judge them correctly, with a recollection of what they are, and also what they are not. They who have enjoyed the privilege of a personal acquaintance with the gayest of our modern humourists—and there are many such (including the present writer) among us still—are best qualified to pronounce an opinion upon this point; and they know how much of darkness and anguish often there is behind the scenes or off the boards. The jokes by or about any given individual do not, after all, amount to a great deal, when they are spread over thirty or forty years : all the genuine sayings of Theodore Hook or Douglas Jerrold would not fill more than a few octavo pages; and these things are to be taken, not as indices to the habitual unbroken mood of the man, but rather as samples of felicity of phrase or thought to be gotten, like mineral ore, under auspicious conditions from a wealthy soil.

We are too grossly subservient to habit and use. We naturally accustom ourselves, unless we reflect, to figure the clown with his tongue perpetually in his cheek and the wit discharging his shafts without cessation or repose—just as, on the contrary, no one would be prepared to believe, without the strongest proof, that a tailor had made a pun, or that a railway porter had written a Greek epigram.

If we try to realise in our imagination Grimaldi stretched on a bed of sickness, a jovial companion in a gouty paroxysm, or an excellent friend, the author of utterances which have delighted and convulsed the stage, in the extremity of mental depression or physical suffering, we ·shall be better able to see that the Anecdote generically, and the Jest in particular, are fortuitous emanations and not parcel of our daily being.

Facetious narrations are too seldom subjected to the test of circumstantial evidence. We are not apt to ask ourselves the question, who delivered the joke, or ushered it into print? There are cases, of course, where the author of a sally or rejoinder himself repeats it to a third party, possibly in its original shape, possibly with embellishments; but there must be, nay, there are numberless instances in which a funny thing is given to a person, not because he said it, but because he might or would have done so. It is an assignment by inference and likelihood.

CHAPTER II.

THE earliest form or phase of the JEST was the product of an illiterate age. A knowledge of the art of writing was a discovery long subsequent to the rise of a taste for the expression of the laughable, for the sake either of amusement or of ridicule. The primitive authors of jokes were men who employed, not the pen, but the chisel and the brush; and the most venerable existing specimens of this branch of human ingenuity belong to art, not to literature; and to Egypt, the cradle and nursery of art.

In his admirable *History of Caricature and Grotesque*, 1865, Wright has accumulated such an immense body of information on this most interesting subject of inquiry that, so far as it goes, it will supersede the necessity for traversing the ground again. He has traced with singular industry and scholarship the growth and development of the jocular sentiment in all its varied points of view, from its first infancy among the Egyptians, through the Greeks and Romans, to modern times and our own country.

For while during centuries the feeling for the grotesque or absurd, together with the almost inborn propensity for the exposure of foibles and vices in an enemy, a rival, or an obnoxious public character, had its outlets only through the agency of art, and the sculptor or draughtsman was the sole resource of those who loved caricature and farce, the introduction of caligraphy by no means diminished the call for the graphic delineators of comedy and satire. The English artists of the

Georgian epoch were equally prolific and unsparing; and even now, when all the civilised communities of the world have their printing presses without number at command, the pencil remains a favourite vehicle for the exhibition of humorous or unpopular traits in distinguished persons of the day, and among many connoisseurs and students a volume of Gillray or Rowlandson is a more welcome object of attention or notice than a printed record.

The engraving has in all ages enjoyed over its literary counterpart or equivalent the great advantage, that it immediately attracts the eye, and enables one to embrace every point of view and the whole story at a glance; whereas in the other case the same effect is scarcely produced on the mind by many pages of letterpress or the most elaborate inscription on metal or stone. The spectator is in fact a far older student than the reader or the listener to a reading, or than the audience of the minstrel of yore. The organs of sight have been the direct media through which innumerable generations of mankind have received all the knowledge and culture which they ever possessed; and we perceive at the present moment how far the cheap print and the gay shop-window go to supply such Englishmen of the nineteenth century as have small leisure and perhaps equally small inclination for books with notions of current sentiments and transactions.

The manuscript or printed page has not a co-ordinate power with the mural sketch or other pictorial representation, with or without its adjunct of hyperbole and broad colouring, in an instantaneous appeal to the passions, or to the sense of the ridiculous, or, again, to the public instinct of wrong. The press bears its part; but whatever its development in the future may prove to be, it will never completely obliterate the demand and admiration for the labours of the graphic illustrator, whose origin is positively lost in antiquity, and whose pursuit was, doubtless, among the subjects of the Rameses dynasty themselves—an accomplishment derived from Oriental (possibly Turanian) instructors; for the most archaic published examples manifest a tolerable intimacy with design and the combination of effect, as well as a capability of awakening hilarious sensations by the burlesque perversion of serious matters.

The joke-wright and the anecdote-monger may be treated as two exceptionally fortunate professional persons, who enter the field of their labours and researches with a light heart and an empty budget. Their accumulation of stock is immense. The capital of all their ancestors becomes their fee simple *ex officio.* There need be among them no struggling beginners, no modest apprenticeship ; and all that is expected at their hands is a certain proficiency in conveyancing, and the addition, before they and the world bid each other farewell, of a donation or two to the bank for the benefit of the public and of ensuing freeholders for evermore.

The introduction of typography, in jocular as in all other branches of literature, was instrumental in accomplishing a transition from oral delivery to the

printed collection.   In lieu of the minstrel
and the *bordeur*, such sections of the
public as could read might have in their
closets and window-recesses garlands of
facetiæ in prose or verse.   The press
slowly superseded the reciter and the
professional buffoon with his budget of
witticisms and tales.   But the process
was of course a very gradual one, so long
as the diffusion of culture remained imperfect and partial ; and for a great length
of time the old-world system of reading
from the MS., or repeating *extempore* to
an audience, and of the passage of jests
and tales from mouth to mouth, continued
more or less to flourish, just as it does
in the form of a revival, among certain
classes of the modern English community,
who seem to do from choice what their
forerunners did from need.

A vein of exaggeration, which is apt
to characterise anecdotes as they are
repeated from mouth to mouth, or transferred from one book to another, resolves
itself into mere innocuous caricature or
gasconade, where the plot is of a comic
turn ; but where a certain indelicacy or

double sense accompanies the original version, the new-renderer has it in his power to pander to the prevailing taste by making a gross story immeasurably more exceptionable, either by simple intensification or by connecting incidents and expressions with persons to whom they never in point of fact belonged.

Now, this I take to be very much the case with the *Jests of Scogin*, a compilation of the Tudor era by a doctor, as it is said, who was guilty of writing a fair amount of matter in a similar vein, but who, if these Jests were truly of his composition, shewed by his *Book of the Introduction of Knowledge*, and one or two other works, that he was capable of something higher. I refer to Doctor Andrew Borde, a learned and ingenious man, as we may perceive, but far from being fastidious in his writings, or (which is worse) in ascribing to the most exalted characters of an antecedent epoch a tolerance of the most outrageous and vulgar buffoonery.

It is exceedingly likely that the court of the susceptible and profligate Edward IV.,

to which Scogin is supposed to have
resorted, was a scene of coarse simplicity
and no model of decorum; and so late
down as the reign of George II. the great
ladies permitted themselves a licence in
speech, which prevented the editor of
Maloniana from printing the whole of
the MS. But so far as the latter circumstance goes, these were mostly passages
inter se (so to speak) ; and it remains
incredible, that some of the adventures
with which Scogin is reported to have
met within the very precincts of the palace,
can have actually happened under the
eyes of the queen and her attendants.
Dr. Borde, I apprehend in fact, has
committed the impropriety of transferring
to another age the manners of his own,
which was so far venial enough, and
consonant with dramatic usage ; but he
has most unwarrantably taken some of
his characters from a sphere of life in
which the enactment of such low pranks
would hardly have been suffered. To
cast aspersions on the representatives
of an extinct dynasty, however, was a
tolerably safe game. *The Jests of Scogin*

had no political significance; and the
occasional reflections on the clergy were
not calculated to give serious offence in
influential quarters, or to Henry VIII.
himself, just at the juncture when the
Reformation was imminent. Not in the
pages of Borde alone, but throughout
the literature of the later part of Henry's
reign, sly strokes at the doomed papal
hierarchy were eyed with evident indulgence and favour. Borde knew his
ground and his customers: had his
satire been levelled at the Government
in an infinitely milder and more covert
way, the stake or the block would have
been his portion; had his book been
published twenty years sooner, his stric-
tures on the Church would scarcely have
been prudent; but he confined his pen,
where he rose above a humble social
level, to names which were little more
than historical, and to an institution
whose days were numbered.

CHAPTER III.

LITERATURE AND THE DRAMA AS CON-
TRIBUTORIES TO JOCULAR LITERATURE
— DEPENDENCE ON SURROUNDINGS
AND CIRCUMSTANCES.

ITERATURE and the Drama
have been the most munificent
contributors to our ANA. If
the sayings reported of or by actors and
authors were subtracted from the grand
total, the residuum would assuredly dis-
play a very deplorable shrinkage ; and
this is easily capable of explanation in a
manner which itself explains the corrupt
form in which much of this lore has
descended to us. For the whole atmosphere of the theatre is conducive to
the suggestion of odd circumstances and
situations, and the professional writer enjoys peculiar facilities, through his reading
and associates, for making himself master

of the good sayings of his own circle
and of other times. As Bacon observed,
"Reading makes a full man, and conversation a ready man"; the caterer for
the stage or the booksellers finds that it
enters into his business to store his brain
with such *bons-mots* and pieces of harmless scandal as he picks up in books or
in society; and these are naturally apt
to undergo, before they reach other ears,
a polishing operation or the action of the
churn. For, as they came to him, they
offended in some particular, perchance,
his artistic eyes, or it seemed good to
change the bill.

To this kind of agency, no doubt, is
owing the large stock, which survives in
print in most languages, of various readings of stories; but a second and very
different influence, not less potential, has
been concurrently at work in the same
direction. From time immemorial the
professional joke-dresser has ranged at
will over the whole field, and kept the
market excellently well supplied with
goods of this special description in every
variety at the lowest possible figure.

Malone, in his *Recollections*, says of Richardson the artist:

"He was a great news and anecdote monger, and in the latter part of his life spent much of his time in gathering and communicating intelligence concerning the King of Prussia, and other topics of the day, as Dr. Burney, who knew him very well, informs me."

This extract furnishes in some degree the key to the origin of a large share of the amusing tales, *jeux d'esprits*, and repartees, which the various extant collections offer to our consideration—that is to say, to their origin *in a second or third state*, as the printseller expresses it; and beyond question, if there is any branch of facetious biography or history which has reached us in an artificial condition, it is *par excellence* that which deals with alleged episodes in the careers of highborn personages, not merely of remote times, but of an approximate generation or so—nay, even of the great folks with whom we might touch elbows, *si fas esset*.

If it be the case that "a jest's prosperity lies in the ear of him that hears it," it is equally true that a pleasantry depends for

its thorough success on the atmosphere in
which it receives utterance, and on the
personality of the narrator. Something
which might seem racy and piquant to an
Oriental, would very probably fall flat in
an ancient Greek and Roman gathering ;
and it demanded all the surrounding costume of Greece or Rome to give salience
and effect to those specimens of wit,
which do not often, as they are recorded,
strike us as remarkably brilliant. It is as
if we put old wine into new bottles. The
liquor is there ; but the crust and the
beeswing have vanished.

So it is with the facetious heritage
which comes to us from our own immediate ancestors. The substance and
outline are with us ; but the setting, the
context, and the *genius loci*, are too frequently to be desired ; and, besides, an
editor has perhaps come upon the ground,
and turned what was rough copy into a
sentence or a paragraph "teres atque
rotundus." It becomes a readable article
of sale ; but it is a sort of handiwork, and
no longer a spontaneous sally or a faithful
report.

On the other hand, it may happen that
a jest bears upon some permanent incidence of human society, and passes with
merely verbal changes from one age, one
language, and one country, to another ;
like the episode mentioned by Lucian in
his *Hetairai*, and likewise by Gellius, of
the lady who, when her admirer sent
her a cask of wine, commending its age,
retorted that it was very small for its age,
—where we observe that the conditions,
being neither local nor temporary, are
capable of universal and perpetual application.

The reduction of pleasantries and satirical thrusts to form must be an outcome
of topographical, climatic and social conditions, and is necessarily dependent on
habits of life, pronunciation, diet, and
dress—nay, on the most trifling minutiæ
connected with national usages.   The
happiness of a witticism or of a taunt
hangs on its relationship at some sort of
angle to the customs and notions prevalent
in a country.   It exists by no other law
than its antagonism or contrast to received
institutions and matters of common belief ;

and hence what in one part of the world
is apt to awaken mirth or resentment, in
another falls flatly on the ear.

The essence and property of a saying
lie under very weighty obligations to local
circumstances and colouring. There can
be no more familiar illustration of my
meaning to an English reader than the
large debt which an Irish or Scottish
piece of humour owes to the Irish or
Scottish brogue. But it has been the same
everywhere from all time. Among the
ancient Greeks an Ionian would have
found much difficulty in appreciating the
point of an Attic sally, while among the
modern Italians a Tuscan would listen
with unmoved countenance to a *jeu
d'esprit* in the Venetian *patois.* The turn
of a syllable, the inflexion of a vowel,
is enough to mar the effect; and a similar
observation holds good of the numberless
dialects spoken throughout the German
Fatherland and the Low Countries.

It is comparatively easy to comprehend
a joke, when there is a well-understood
acceptation of terms and a community of
atmosphere and costume ; but to study

these matters at a distance both of time
and place, and to have to allow for altered
circumstances or surroundings is immeasurably more difficult ; and this is
what I do not think we always remember
that we have to do in estimating the good
things of our own precursors on this soil,
and still more those of individuals governed
in all their ways of thinking and acting by
considerations which we can never perfectly bring home to ourselves.

Taking the United States, again, the
same expression will be treated in one
part as of obnoxious significance ; in another it will perhaps raise a smile ; and in
a third it will bear no meaning whatever.

CHAPTER IV.

JUSTIFICATION FOR THE PRESENT UNDER-
TAKING—LITERARY INTEREST OF THE
SUBJECT—THE VARIOUS CLASSES OF
JEST—THE SERIOUS ANECDOTE THE
ORIGINAL TYPE AND THE JEST AN
EVOLUTION — GREEK AND ROMAN
EXAMPLES—THE "DEIPNOSOPHISTÆ"
OF ATHENÆUS.

A JUSTIFICATION for the present inquiry may be found,
then, in the historical, biographical and literary interest with which it
abounds, and in the multiplicity of aspects
under which the topic is capable of being
contemplated.

The Jest resembles a tree of many
branches. It is couched in a wide variety
of shapes—namely, the Riddle, the Epigram, the Apologue or Tale, the Repartee,
the Quibble, and the Pun.

Of these, the Apologue and the Riddle are the most ancient—the latter being entitled to priority, if we take into account its positive origin in the Hebrew Scriptures themselves, although the jocular or comic development is so much more recent. The same criticism applies to the Apologue which was transplanted from Oriental soil, where it has ever been a favourite method of conveying instruction and amusement, into the oldest Western vehicles for the same twofold purpose, such as the *Gesta Romanorum*, the *Fables* of Æsop, and *Reynard the Fox*. These productions, with many others, were designed as a method of inculcating moral precepts and political lessons under a fictitious or romantic garb. The facetious adaptation was a later growth, and first manifests itself in the French and Latin *fabliaux* in prose or verse edited for us by Méon and Wright.

Next in the scale of antiquity to the Apologue and Riddle we may be warranted in ranking the Epigram; and this, too, like the two others to which I have been referring, was in its inception and early employment satirical rather than burlesque for the

most part. Humour did not enter at first
into its composition or design. Any one
who looks through the Greek Anthology
may see that the productions in that lan
guage are serious narratives treated in a
terse and condensed style.

The Quibble and Repartee were tolerably popular features and characteristics
in the jest-books of the seventeenth century, when the formation of literary clubs,
and the increased correspondence between
men of parts and wit, naturally led to the
growth of that large body of sayings which
the printed and MSS. collections have
handed down to us. The age immediately succeeding that of Shakespear
saw the uprise of the quip and crank, and
the retort courteous, " conceits, clinches,
flashes, and whimzies," and all the rest
of the merry, motley company. Such
utterances they were as undoubtedly appealed with success to their auditors and
readers ; but so thorough is the change
which has stolen over our taste and feeling
in these matters, that, in turning over the
leaves of a volume of *facetiæ*, which was
once read with avidity and delight, the

impression now produced is a mingled one of surprise and disappointment.

The humorous literature, like the coinage, of a particular era, seems as if it were part of it; and it is in a vast majority of instances incapable of assimilation or transfer, as I shall endeavour to prove by a few casual selections from miscellanies which were in prime vogue and favour when James I. was on the throne, and those three renowned hostelries, the Mermaid, the Mitre, and the Devil, were flourishing centres of all that was cultivated and spiritual.

The serious Anecdote naturally took precedence of its jocular evolution or offspring; and indeed the latter, as is obvious enough, could hardly exist as a congener, till artificial and more or less complicated forms of social life had been developed. Even the entries in such books as Plutarch, where he narrates some incident in the biography of one of his heroes of a nature less grave than usual, and of a sufficiently playful or salient nature to have tempted the editors of the ancient collections of *facetiæ* to include them in their pages, cannot quite properly be said to be exceptions to the rule, that the Jest, as we understand it, was unknown to the ancients, although all civilised nations have in their turn possessed a keen sense of the laughable, and have devised methods of holding up to derision those who deviated from the prevailing standard of decorum, morality, or etiquette; or, again, who exposed themselves to personalities from special causes.

The selections from classic sources in the *Merry Tales and Quick Answers*, printed in the time of Henry VIII., have on this account a tendency to weight the book, and render it less attractive and readable at the present time than its famous contemporary, entitled *A Hundred Merry Tales*, which was prepared on a more judicious principle, and excluded all but tales of more or less current interest.

The favourite Greek and Roman authors with compilers of *Ana* have been at all periods Plutarch, Aulus Gellius, Lucian, Athenæus, and Diogenes Laertius. It is very rarely that Homer or Cicero is enlisted in their service by the caterers

3

for popular entertainment; and even in the case of the *Merry Tales and Quick Answers* the stories about the ancients are appended at the end, as if they had been an afterthought or a stratagem for making out the copy.

There is a coincidence between Lucian and Athenæus in this respect,—that the *jeux d'esprit*, such as they are, in both writers occur almost exclusively in their remarks on Courtesans; and we ought to be the less surprised at such a circumstance, when we call to mind that the Greek *hetairai* were precisely the class which chiefly mixed with men of wit, and was most apt to yield subject-matter for pleasant sallies and epigrammatic clinches. Among the Romans, too, as we easily collect from the writings of their amatory poets and the lighter productions of Horace, the women of pleasure were accomplished and attractive; but no type exactly parallel to the Greek *hetaira*, as she is depicted in the pages of literary history, seems ever to have existed in Italy, and the nearest approach to her socially is perhaps the Parisian grisette, and, in point of culture and mental qualities, the gay female throng which haunted the court of Charles II. Both these, however, were, while presenting features of resemblance, essentially dissimilar from their prototype, who was a natural emanation of the climate, government, and moral atmosphere in which she was born and bred.

Notwithstanding the undoubted presence of a feeling for humour among the Greeks and other remote nationalities, one finds it possible to lay down the *Deipnosophistæ* and the *Hetairæ* with an unrelaxed countenance; and one arrives at the conclusion that all the best things have perished, or that much of the comic effect produced at table or on the stage was due to local costume and to evanescent gesture and pantomime,—just as the triumphs of Grimaldi and Liston among ourselves, and Richard Tarlton before them, depended so materially on personal mannerism and *extempore* grimace.

In Lucian the most remarkable specimen, and that which has been most frequently quoted and borrowed, is the retort of the lady to her lover about the small size of the cask of wine which he had sent to her, considering its reputed age; and this is also in the *Deipnosophistæ*, where it is related, however, of Phryne.

Perhaps the most interesting feature in the latter work, in connection with the immediate topic, is the notice which we get of the Athenian Club of the SIXTY, in the time of Demosthenes. Even the names or *sobriquets* of some of the members have survived; and Philip of Macedon honoured the institution by the expression of his regret that his other avocations precluded him from joining it, and by a simultaneous request that a collection of all the good sayings uttered at its gatherings should be sent to him. Whether or not this flattering requisition was supplied, there is no record; but in any case it shadows the possibility of a jest-book far more ancient, and presumably also more copious, than that of Hierocles.

It thus appears, moreover, that the earliest companionship of anecdotes of all descriptions is with the feast and the cup ; the lost conversational gems of the Attic Sexagint were distilled over the convivial glass ; and the pages of Athenæus are put forward in like manner as the gradual progeny of table-talk— table-talk which may have received in not a few instances the polishing touches of an editor.

The student who may be at the pains to consult the *Deipnosophistæ* and its analogues will probably concur with me in the opinion that such repositories were little calculated to prove advantageous resorts for later compilers of *bons-mots*. Not merely is it that the bulk of the matter is not with ease transfusible into a modern language, but the spirit and atmosphere of these effusions are foreign to our sympathies; and the wittiest sayings of the wittiest of Corinthian humourists, male or female, are apt to strike us, not having the context, as vapid and pointless.

Athenæus has preserved several of the repartees of Gnathæna, the celebrated courtesan. One of the best of them appears to be her play upon words, when Pausanius, who was nicknamed *Laccus*, fell into a cask, and she remarked that the cellar (*laccus*) had fallen into the cask. Another is by no means contemptible. "Once, when a chattering fellow was relating that he had just come from the Hellespont, 'Why, then,' said she, 'did you not go to the first city in that country?' and when he asked what city, 'To Sigeum,' said she." But in a third, which occurs immediately below, the salt is very thinly sprinkled:—

"On one occasion, when Chærephon came to sup with her without an invitation, Gnathæna pledged him in a cup of wine. 'Take it,' said she, 'you proud fellow!' 'I proud?' 'Who can be more so,' said she, 'when you come without even being invited?'"

Here is one of another *hetaira*, Nico by name:—

"Once, when she met a parasite, who was very thin in consequence of a long sickness, she said to him, 'How lean you are!' 'No wonder,' says he, 'for what do you think is all I have had to eat these three days?' 'Why, a leather bottle,' says she, 'or perhaps your shoes.'"

Our author adduces these and several other ineptitudes of similar calibre in

honest good faith, and assures us that
the lady was always very neat and witty
in all she said. He adds that she com-
piled a code of laws for banquets, in
compliance with which her friends were
required to pay their respects to her and
her daughters ; but these regulations have
not been preserved. It is to be hoped
that they were wiser than her jocular
achievements.

The same criticism is, in the main,
applicable to the gossip which Athenæus
has bequeathed to us about three other
distinguished members of the sisterhood
—Lais, Glycera and Thais. One of these
items concerns, however, the dramatist
Menander, and awakens an independent
interest :—

"Once, when Menander the poet had failed
with one of his plays, and came to her house,
Glycera brought him some milk, and recommended him to drink it. But he said he would
rather not, for there was some γραῦς in it, that
word signifying either an old woman or the scum
on milk. But she replied, ' Blow it away, and
take what there is beneath.'"

There is a second anecdote, which

deserves attention, apart from any merit
of its own, because it illustrates the very
ancient symbolism of the seal or signet,
which survived down to modern times :—

"A lover of hers once sent his seal to Lais the
Corinthian, and desired her to come to him. But
she said, 'I cannot come ; it is only clay !'"

A certain dramatic interest centres in
the famous Phryne, whose adventure in a
court of justice is so well known. There
is a story that her contemporary, the courtesan Gnathæna aforesaid, once twitted
her with her dulness, insinuating that her
wit ought to be sharpened on a whetstone;
but assuredly the two subjoined bits are
quite as good as anything that is cited of
Gnathæna herself :—

"Once, when a slave, who had been flogged,
was giving himself airs as a young man towards
her, and saying that he had been often entangled,
she pretended to look vexed ; and when he asked
her the reason, 'I am jealous of you,' said she,
'because you have been so often smitten.'"

"A very covetous lover of hers was coaxing
her, and saying to her, 'You are the Venus of
Praxiteles.' 'And you,' said she, playing on the
double meaning of the sculptor's name, 'are the
Cupid of Phidias.'"

Turning from the fair sex to that which claims no such distinction, we do not find ourselves face to face with any improvement in quality. The following is quoted by Athenæus from Xenophon :—

"Philip the jester, having knocked at the door, told the boy who answered, to tell the guests who he was, and that he was desirous to be admitted ; and he said that he came provided with everything which could qualify him for supping at other people's expense."

Take another, the pith of which resides in the twofold circumstance that Lysimachus had two prime favourites, Bithys and Paris, and that the performers on the comic stage had, as a rule, short names : —

"Demetrius Poliorcetes was a man very eager for anything which could make him laugh, as Phylarchus tells us in the sixth book of his History. And he it was who said, that the palace of Lysimachus was in no respect different from a comic theatre, for that there was no one there bigger than a dissyllable."

So Athenæus ; but the particular citation goes rather to prove that Demetrius endeavoured to provoke mirth in others, and that if he succeeded in this instance,

the risible organs of his friends must have
been almost painfully sensitive. Thus
much it appeared almost indispensable to
furnish by way of warranty for what had
been said just before in disparagement of
the ancient school of humour.

Nor are the examples cited by Athenæus
under *Parodies*, which might seem at first
blush to belong to the same genus or
family, more felicitous or impressive.
There, as in the other sections devoted
to *Courtesans* and *Jesters*, the double
meaning and the quibble preponderate,
and some of the points demand a solution
which nearly amounts to a gloss or an
essay. There is positively nothing worth
copying.

But I have entered into these details
because I can then finally dismiss the
Deipnosophistæ, which offers no parallels
to the modern *Ana*, save and except the
hackneyed tale of the little cask of great
age, which Taylor, the Water Poet, in his
Wit and Mirth, applies to "a proper
gentlewoman" in his own rather clumsy
fashion.

Of semi-serious epigrams in prose-form

the author of the *Deipnosophistæ* supplies
us with at least one noteworthy specimen,
where he speaks of Myrtilus as discours-
ing on every subject as if he had studied
that alone. This fine sentiment is akin to
the description of Aristippus :—

"Omnis Aristippum decuit color et status et res,"

and to the "Nihil tetigit quod non
ornavit," which has been applied to our
Goldsmith.

The epigram is by nature and necessity
unliteral. It is an *ex-officio* extravagance
or hyperbole, from which you must take
a liberal discount. One of the mediæval
worthies, Alanus ab Insulis, was desig-
nated the *Universal Doctor.* It was a
complimentary *façon de parler.*

We are here somehow reminded of the
account which Macaulay makes Charles II.
give of Sydney Godolphin, that he was
such an excellent courtier, "because he
was never in the way, and never out of
the way."

Then, again, we get it in such forms
as "the Admirable Crichton," "Single-
Speech Hamilton," "Capability Brown,"

or " Athenian Stuart," where a real or
reputed specialism is summed up in
a word. So that the editor of books of
epigrams, who does not go beyond the
ordinary familiar types, leaves a good deal
of the field unreaped.

The *Deipnosophistæ* constituted a work,
which most naturally suggested to mediæval and later compilers miscellanies
fórmed on an analogous . basis, but
adapted from time to time to the chang-
ing demands of public taste. The most
remarkable of these productions, perhaps,
was the *Mensa Philosophica*, of which
the authorship is a matter of dispute,
but which was constructed to some extent
out of the *Saturnalia* of Macrobius, and
of which there is an Elizabethan counterpart, entitled *The Schoolmaster or Teacher
of Table Philosophy*. This, and the
Convivial Discourses elsewhere mentioned,
seem to breathe the air of a social system,
when men lingered over the dinner or
supper table, or adjourned, as was not
unusual, after the actual meal to indulge
in wine and conversation.

I shall now proceed to treat the

Greek Anthology, the *Noctes Atticæ*, and the *Lives of the Philosophers*, which, like Lucian and Athenæus, are simply of value as the foundations and pioneers of the class of literature which I am examining, and as introductory to the leading purpose in view. It must become evident that the sources of the vein of wit which pervades modern literature and society is to be sought elsewhere—in circumstances and conditions of life altogether different—in our political development, climate and blood.

CHAPTER V.

THE "NOCTES ATTICÆ" — PECULIAR
    VALUE OF THE WORK—THE "LIVES
    OF THE PHILOSOPHERS," BY DIOGENES
    LAERTIUS—CHARACTER OF THE BOOK
    —THE GOLDEN TRIPOS.

O the same class of production as
the *Deipnosophistæ* belongs the
Attic Nights of Aulus Gellius.
The information which the latter affords
is kindred in scope and character;
and, though somewhat less voluminous,
it is almost equally multifarious and
discursive. But the *Noctes Atticæ* did
not profess, like the others, to be the
offspring of an imaginary scheme, in the
same way as the *Decameron* and the
Arabian Nights; its pages preserve to us,
and to all who come after us, the literary
Collectanea of a Roman jurist, scholar

and antiquary, and it will remain for ever one of the most delightful and instructive of books in any language or any literature. It is certainly remarkable that the same obscurity which surrounds the personal history of Diogenes Laertius hangs over that of the Roman. That they both lived about the same time, in the first or second century of our era, seems to be settled ; but a clear approximation, much less any biographical *minutiæ*, are not forthcoming in either case.

Some few matters the two writers exhibit in common ; which is the less surprising when we consider their nearness in time to each other, and bear in mind the plan on which Gellius at least worked. His preface commences thus :—

"More pleasing works than the present may certainly be found ; but my object in writing this was to provide my children as well as myself with that kind of amusement in which they might properly relax and indulge themselves, at the intervals from more important business. . . . Whatever book came into my hand, *whether it was Greek or Latin,* or whatever I heard that was either worthy of being recorded or agreeable to my fancy, I wrote down without distinction and without order."

The result to us is, that we possess such a commonplace book as stands fairly by itself without a rival, looking at its date, in Roman literature, in the same way that Athenæus does in Greek.

It would not be possible to offer a complete introductory survey of the subject under consideration without turning back to see what the sources were to which later wits would resort—without inspecting the basement of the edifice, so to speak. Otherwise, vastly interesting as they are on literary and archæological grounds, such relics of antiquity as Athenæus and Gellius yield mainly pure Anecdota in the strict acceptation of the term. The pages of the former are more redolent of the theatre and the gymnasium ; those of the author of the *Attic Nights* breathe the atmosphere of the study, and where he tells a story of some *hetaira* or dancing-girl, he cites his original. But Gellius has devoted much of his space to topics which were more congenial than the adventures and amours of the gay folks

of or about the time; he is more profuse
on philological dissertation, serious pieces
of personal history, and points relevant
to the general costume of the Rome
which he knew. Now and then, but not
so often as might have been expected
and excused, the lawyer peeps out. Here
and there, too, he reminds us of the
Deipnosophistæ, as in the twenty-second
section, which opens with an account of
the conversation and readings which took
place at the table of Favorinus; and the
very following chapter is occupied by a
sample of dramatic criticism, in which
his opinion is given of some Roman play
founded on the Greek comedians, as we
now adapt pieces for the stage from the
French.

It is a most strangely heterogeneous,
and at the same time most charming,
miscellany, lacking which our knowledge
of Roman literature, society and manners
would be far less complete. But, as it
has been already indicated in a general
way of all the books of the sub-classical
period, the *Noctes Atticæ* does not prove
of great service to the gatherer of *facetiæ*;

4

and the few scattered trifles of that nature which the work contains would not be held of sufficient consequence to find a place in a modern collection. Such as they are, they occur for the most part in the early jest-books, and are precisely such as an editor nowadays would instinctively skip as out of keeping with present notions and demands.

This fact tends to substantiate the position which I have asserted, that our ideas of wit and humour are widely and essentially different from those of the ancients; for it is only, I apprehend, in this single particular that Gellius fails to keep touch with us. He is in most respects, like all eminent writers, remarkably modern and contemporary ; and, as a rule, the matters which he judged worth writing down so many centuries ago, we read with gratitude and enjoyment.

The Lives of the Philosophers, by Diogenes Laertius, is a very familiar title and even book. But it is at the same time almost to be regarded and taken as the prototype of literary works based, with every wish on the part of the writer

to be accurate and veracious, on hearsay
and tradition. Diogenes is the Greek
Aubrey. His transactions in conjecture
and conflicting opinions are marvellously
large; and, as a consequence, his text
abounds with uncertainty and confusion.
One is reminded nearly at every page of
the story of the Southern gentleman who
once undertook a journey to the High-
lands of Scotland to inquire for *Meester
Grant*; and, singularly enough, the source
of the difficulty is very much the same.
Diogenes made himself the biographer
of a people whose choice of names was
limited, and among whom the same name
was of common occurrence. So long as
the men themselves lived, it signified little
or nothing; but if they became famous
and historical, or if one out of several
did so, the facilities for mixture of
identity were, as a matter of course,
immense. This circumstance, which is
not casual, but is the rule *not* proving
the exception, sensibly diminishes the
value of the *Lives* as an authority; and
it is easy to see how the taint has been
communicated to the best of our modern

Cyclopædias, where the contributors of
articles are obliged to own repeatedly,
that some fact or other is attributed by
half a dozen ancient writers to as many
different persons of the same name,
nationality and approximate period.

I shall pass over the circumstance that
the biography of Diogenes is almost as
involved and obscure as his text, for I
am merely dealing with him and his
celebrated book in a prefatory way.   I
should be very sorry indeed to undervalue
such a unique and fascinating magazine
of gossip and tradition ; nor have I at
present to concern myself with the con-
tradictory statements, not only about men
of inferior fame, but about such pro-
minent characters as Thales and Plato ;
and, besides, in relation to the most
important events of their careers and the
points most vital to their reputation.

Take, for instance, in the account of
Thales, the well-aired anecdote of the
Golden Tripos.   I quote from the old
English translation.   " As for what is
recorded," says he, " concerning the
Tripos found out by the fishermen, and

sent to the *Wise Men* by the *Milesians*,
it still remains an undoubted Truth." He
then narrates this "undoubted truth ";
and when he has done so, he successively
furnishes three other versions materially
differing; and we have to go only a
step further, when we encounter a saying
of Thales as to his gratitude for three
things—that he was a man, and not a
beast; that he was a man, and not a
woman ; and that he was a Greek, and
not a barbarian—which, it seems, is as
likely to have been a saying of Socrates.
We have all heard something very similar
of Dr. Parr and Sir James Mackintosh.

These discrepancies are very thickly
sown throughout the *Lives*, and throughout those of whom it might be conceived
that, in the time at least of Diogenes,
something like authentic and consistent
information would have been preserved
in Greece, at all events regarding salient
facts. Yet between the era of the biographer and that of many, if not most,
of his subjects, the lapse of years was
more than sufficient, in the absence of
systematic records, to accumulate a vast

amount of error and entanglement, especially when so many individuals of the
same name flourished about the same
date. We perceive that even as to the
number of the Wise Men, and who they
were, there is a conflict of opinion. But,
on the other hand, in his memoir of
Solon, Diogenes is remarkably minute,
and supplies us with the very words
which he employed in addressing the
Athenian Assembly and the texts of
several letters written to contemporaries,
which, to be just, he does also in the
case of Thales. His tone, however, in
the life of Solon is more confident; and
he does not trouble himself or us with
parallel traditions and various readings.
We may discern equally strong ground
for scepticism here and there; but he
felt his footing surer, as Homer, in some
parts of the Odyssey, evidently writes
from report, and in others from personal
information. Where, as he does so freely
in the case of Thales and others, he lays
before us all the theories about an event
or a fact, Diogenes reminds us of Hero-
dotus, who so often absolves himself from

responsibility by setting down all the accounts which had reached him, and leaving us to pick out the truth among them.

A considerable proportion of the aphorisms ascribed to the Wise Men strike us as rather commonplace ; but that may be the result of familiarity. James I. observed that he was a bold man who first ate an oyster ; but the attributes of strangeness and courage have alike ceased to exist. Perhaps one of the maxims which still most preserves its verdure is that of Pittacus of Mitylene : *To observe the season,* which is just our Selden's *Distingue tempora.*

The anecdotes with which the pages of Diogenes are plentifully illustrated are, as I have hinted, familiar to the point of indifference ; and I believe that they almost invariably suffer from translation into a foreign idiom and epoch. If we are scarcely able to relish the good things which passed current in our own country in the days of the Tudors and the Stuarts, what likelihood is there of a cordial sympathy with such fragments of the wit and wisdom as have survived of men who lived at such an immeasurably greater distance of time under wholly different conditions and influences? From an historical and philosophical point of view we try to make the best of them; but jocularly they amount to very little indeed.

CHAPTER VI.

THE GREEK ANTHOLOGY—GREEK EPI-
GRAMS—HERODOTUS—ARISTOPHANES
—PLATO.

THE GREEK ANTHOLOGY offers to our view, in the main, a body of national sentiment and local costume. The witticisms or smart turns are generally so much a part of the life of the country and period to which they immediately appertain, that an English reader might be apt scarcely to become aware of their true drift, of the inner satirical or humorous sense in the mind and intention of their composers, if he could forget that he had under his eyes the most important productions of ancient Hellas in the way of Epigram and Epigrammatic Inscription collected together for his edification and amusement.

It is perfectly natural and fit that the facetious literature of the Greeks should partake in tone and odour of the genius, climate and society which produced it. We may not appreciate a Greek joke, because the train of associations is broken; but if it does not come home to us exactly as it was meant by the author, it remains as a contributory factor to our knowledge of a never - to - be - forgotten people.

All that I seek to urge here is, that the English school of wit has barely any archaic foreign *substrata*, but is, to a very large and leading extent, as my learned American acquaintance, Mr. Phelps, lately observed of our law, a product of the region which gave it birth and development. There are certain broad and general features common to all humanity at all times, and independent of conditions and place :—

   " One touch of nature makes the whole world
      kin,"

and there are cases, of course, where the same happy thought has presented itself *bonâ fide* to different persons at different periods, to men chronologically and geographically as far removed as an Athenian of the age of Pericles and an Englishman of the age of George III. The same circumstances have a proneness to gravitate to the same issues, where it is some normal trait of human nature that is concerned, or some incident of habitual recurrence.

But the pages of this Greek Anthology, of which I employ for convenience the ordinary English version, have to be winnowed in the same proportion as those of the other classical or quasi-classical books which we have just left behind us, in order to extract matter which is perfectly intelligible without the context. For everybody must feel that a translation has no chemical virtue beyond the exchange of terms. A Greek epigram, in nine instances out of ten, is a Greek epigram none the less though it be clothed in an English dress. It is like a keyless cipher, unless the reader takes up the volume where it occurs with a mastery of the surrounding conditions, which nine Englishmen out of ten do not possess.

On the other hand, how free from temporary feeling and interest are some of the flowers in this poetical chaplet! How superior to all the mutations and vicissitudes which the land of their birth has since suffered! Their motto is *Perennis et fragrans.*

Take a few illustrations :—

"Said the lame to the blind, 'On your back let
      me rise';
   So the eyes were the legs, and the legs were
      the eyes."

"A fool, bitten by many fleas, put out the light saying, 'You no longer see me.'"

"Why do you fruitlessly wash the body of an Indian? Forbear your art."

"The thin Diophantus, once wishing to hang himself, laid hold of a spider's web, and strangled himself."

"Pheidon neither drenched me nor touched me; but, being ill of a fever, I remembered his name, and died."

A more pungent jest on a doctor was

never uttered, perhaps, than this ! Nor
would it be easy to discover in our modern
collections more telling and ingenious skits
than the two next :

> " 'Tis said that certain death awaits
>   The raven's nightly cry ;
> But at the sound of Cymon's voice
>   The very ravens die."

> " Lazy Mark, snug in prison, in prison to stay,
> Thought confessing a murder the easiest way."

Then how true to character and how
permanent are such epigrammatic *jeux
d'esprit* as these !

> "ON A STATUE OF NIOBE.

> " The gods to stone transformed me ; but again
> I from Praxiteles new life obtain."

> "Though to your face that mirror lies,
>   'Tis just the glass for you ;
> Demosthenes, you'd shut your eyes,
>   If it reflected true."

> " Some say, Nycilla, that you dye your hair—
> Those jet black locks—you bought them at a
>   fair ; "

which is exactly the modern quatrain :

> " The lovely hair, which Celia wears,
>> Is hers: who would have thought it ?—
> She swears 'tis hers, and true she swears ;
>> For I know where she bought it."

Plato is made to say of a statue : " Diodorus put to sleep this satyr, not carved it " ; and Lucian is accredited with the *mot* that " it were easier to find white crows and winged tortoises than an orator of repute in Cappadocia."

We come to an item, where Shakespear was unconsciously forestalled by an epigrammatist who lived eleven centuries before him—Palladas the grammarian :—

> " This life a theatre we well may call,
>> Where every actor must perform with art :
> Or laugh it through, and make a farce of all,
>> Or learn to bear with grace his tragic part."

The old English proverb, " Building is a sweet impoverishing," has its prototype in the couplet :—

> " The broad highway to poverty and need
> Is much to build and many mouths to feed."

But a second strikes the imagination as equally native and verdant, from the supreme faculty which is resident in men of first-rate genius of maintaining their proximity to each successive age :—

> " The Muses to Herodotus one day
>   Came, nine of them, and dined ;
> And in return, their host to pay,
>   Each left a book behind."

It cannot be predicated of what follows that the lapse of years has impaired its application :—

> "A boy was crowning the monument of his step-mother, thinking that her temper had been changed.   But the stone, falling, killed the child, while he leaned on the grave.   Shun, ye children, even the grave of a step-mother."

There is an epigram on a miser, who calculated, while he was ill in bed, that it would cost a drachma more to live than to die, and refused to see a physician ; and a second on a bad poet and a clumsy surgeon, of whom it is said that they had destroyed more persons than " the waters in the time of Deucalion, or than Phaeton, who burned up those upon the earth."

The *Anthology* is of a mingled yarn, like our own Miscellanies, in which the most delicate wit and the broadest fun so fre-

quently find themselves next neighbours.
The pair which I subjoin belongs to the
former and higher category :—

> " The Muses, seeking for a shrine,
>   Whose glories ne'er should cease,
> Found, as they stray'd, the soul divine
>   Of Aristophanes."

> "Three are the Graces.   Thou wert born to be
> The Grace that serves to grace the other three."

The first of these is ascribed to Plato,
who was better prepared to relish, than
we can be reasonably asked to do, the
faithful and diverting reflections of contemporary life and Greek human nature
from the pens of the dramatists of his
country.   The value of such masterpieces
as literary compositions and pictures of
manners remains unaltered and unalter-
able ; but upon us the comic strokes and
the byplay are almost lost.   Nor would
it be possible to fill a small volume with
bons-mots from the Greek Theatre, likely to
appeal with success to the existing market.
For the elements of popularity are clearly
and naturally hostile to its endurance ; and
the narrow extent of the exceptions proves

the rule. The bulk of our own popular
literature of all kinds is *feuille-morte* ; and
no artificial reproduction can make it
otherwise than archæologically instructive.
To reprint a book which is dead is to
make it die twice.

Out of these *Lives of Philosophers*,
this *Table-Talk* of Athenæus, these *Attic
Nights*, and this *Florilegium* of satire and
wit, the *Anthology*, what sort of sum-total
does the harvestman gather in ? But
unless by a strange accident the best
specimens of the Greek Muse in the
present direction or department have unexceptionally disappeared, these must have
constituted the staple material with which
the Athenian Club of the *Sixty* amused
themselves and their correspondents.

The story about Philip and his connection with this body perhaps sets the father
of Alexander before some of us in a rather
new light, and in a more favourable one
than other anecdotes which are associated
with his name. By the way, that where
the poor woman is made to appeal from
Philip drunk to Philip sober, strikes us
as having more than a jocular value—as

5

betokening the primitive condition of judicial forms in Macedon at that period.

It forms by no means the least singular of survivals that the names of several of the members of the Sixty Club have been preserved—just a tenth, including that of one who was nicknamed the *Lobster*. The Sixty were to Athenian society what the Literary Club was to London in the days of Reynolds and Johnson—possibly more; for it was a greater novelty and a fresher influence. But the Literary Club itself was far more than the successor of other institutions, of which earlier men, like Beaumont and Dryden, Addison and Steele, had been the ornament and the life.

The modern manner of epigrammatic wit may be intrinsically similar to that of the Greeks, but certainly diverges from it widely enough in point of detail and colour. I am only at present, however, dealing with the *principia* of the subject, and shewing, as well as I can, to what extent the ancients laid the foundations of the wealth in this branch of culture of which we find ourselves the possessors.

But the strong influence of local atmo-

sphere and idiom is illustrated by that
epigram of Burns to Mr. Ferguson :—

> " The king's poor blackguard slave am I,
>   And scarce dare spare a minute ;
> But I'll be wi' you by-and-by,
>   Or else the devil's in it ; "

which strikes both sides of the Tweed as
intelligible and clever, but would have
fallen as flatly on the ear of a Greek as
some of the traditional sayings in Athenæus, at which the Sixty would have
clapped their hands, do on that of a
modern Englishman.

The epigram lends itself with tolerable
readiness to the service of the joking
guild, and the rhythmical form often
communicates an elegance of turn and a
happiness of finish not reachable in prose.
The distich of Dr. Joseph Warton on the
aphorism of his friend Dr. Balguy, *that
wisdom was sorrow*, is to the point here:—

> " If what you advance, dear Doctor, be true,
>   That wisdom is sorrow, how wretched are
>   you ! "

where in a couplet we see combined jest,
sentiment, and philosophy : a sparkling

antithesis and a compliment worthy of Pope.

Sometimes the epigrammatic jest of later days confines itself to mere verbal quibble ; as, for instance :—

> " The French have taste in all they do,
>   Which we are quite without ;
> For nature, which to them gave *goût*,
>   To us gave only gout."

A small thesis on international pronunciation, for which its metric dress partly helps as a passport : how lamely it would read in prose !

CHAPTER VII.

FORMULATION OF THE JEST—EDITORIAL
TREATMENT OF STORIES—SOPHISTI-
CATED VERSIONS.

THE literary formulation of the Jest, though it seems to be a matter which should go without saying, is, on the contrary, an aspect of the inquiry which presents itself least of all to the mind of the student. The best artificial anecdote in point of structure is apt to be edited material, and does not come to our hands, as a rule, *ipsissimis verbis,* or in the stage of raw unmanufactured goods. For jokes are customarily delivered by the author rough, as it were, from the quarry, and before they are admissible into type have to undergo certain occult scientific processes known to experts—have to pass through the alembic.

The cue having been given, it does
not demand much analytical acumen to
discern in the majority of entries in a
jest-book the hand behind the scenes,
the artist's touch.   It becomes fairly easy
to detect the fact that the joke, whatever
it is, has not reached the pages which
it is intended to enrich direct from the
lips of the utterer, but has been in
the finisher's laboratory. Something in the
texture of the sentence, or maybe in the
wording, seemed to call for amendment.
There are cases where, by rounding
a corner or sharpening an edge, the
dramatic beauty of a *mot* is enhanced
beyond common credibility.

This species of manipulation is one
from which originals are calculated to
suffer in the ratio of their linear extent ;
or, in other words, the briefer a jest is,
the less likely it is to encounter the
transforming or embellishing agency of
an editor in ambush. Such monosyllabic
flashes as Theodore Hook and Douglas
Jerrold were accustomed to discharge on
the spur of the moment afford a certain
likelihood of being pure from the makers ;

and, so far as Jerrold at all events is
concerned, there are many still living
who were absolute earwitnesses of some
of his happiest efforts in this way. His
perception and grasp were almost electric
in their rapidity; and the evenings at the
Club, of which he was the co-founder and
glory, must rank among the pleasantest
recollections of such as had the good
fortune to be present.

A curious article might be written, if
such a thing were feasible, on the progress of jests and allied productions from
the mouths of the authors to the printed
page, with a view of the strange scientific
processes employed in adapting the rough
material for publication. Men of wit
are, as a rule, not men of letters, or
even persons of literary training and ex-
perience; and the *prima stamina* or
germs of their most felicitous utterances
and most interesting anecdotes are always
apt to require the hand of the *redacteur*.
There is almost inevitably something in
the first draft or skeleton of a *bon
mot*, or a choice piece of gossip, which
a critical eye will detect as inimical to

its popularity, as well as to the reputation
of the *conteur*. The editor is the middle-
man between the manufacturer and the
public. He knows better than the former
what he really meant, and better than
anybody what the latter will find palat-
able. As genuine sherry is too bitter to
be used without a blend, so the *ipsissima
verba* of the jocular oracle are most
frequently treated as a *nucleus* or a cue;
and the upshot is a description of mosaic,
in which the respective claims of wit and
editor are no longer apportionable. The
fruitful outpourer of good sayings may
have ceased to rank among living celebrities, and the scintillations of his genius
are gathered into the workshop; or, if he
scatters his treasures during his life, like
a prodigal, among his familiars, it is a
marvel if there are not one or two deft
hands waiting to dress the nuggets for
the market, and even to wrap them up
so adroitly, that their own father would
scarcely recognise them ! If the strict
truth could be ascertained, there are
hundreds of jokes floating in the social
atmosphere, which bear to their actual

makers a relationship cognate to that between Dame Partlet and the duckling.

Even the merest quips and puns, however, are not exempt from the profanation of the garbler. He mars them, not in the stealing, but in the transcription or report. He is joke-proof, or he misses the point by a hair. He builds an arch, and does not see that he has forgotten the keystone. This criticism holds good both of Jerrold and Charles Lamb, two men who have never been surpassed in their astonishing mastery of the *mot* in its real meaning and compass. Yet some of Lamb's happiest hits have been robbed of their vitality by the neglect on the part of his biographers of that nicety which is so imperative in the registration of these casual traits. To omit, alter, or modify a single word is nothing less than sacrilege and death—sacrilege to the author and death to his performance. "Oh," the culprit on conviction may tell you, "the gist is the same; there is no substantial difference." Let him take his discretion back. Is a common carrier to foist changelings upon us?

The revision of *jeux d'esprit* for the sake of augmented effect may be more or less venial; and where the primary object is to amuse, and no vital chord is touched, the reduction of details to an intelligible and impressive shape is possibly a benefit to the public, which might not appreciate the account unground and unpolished. There are so many hazards and drawbacks attendant on *vivâ-voce* delivery; and the editor, after all, only stands to the humourist in a parallel relation to that which the reporter occupies towards parliamentary proceedings. He does not render them precisely as he had 'them from the' speakers' mouths, but as the latter would have given them if they had had the opportunity of correcting the proofs. It virtually amounts to an extension of the authority of literature over unwritten matter. The substance and the quantity are preserved, like liquid poured from a tankard into a saucer; but the component parts have changed places, and the record is drafted and printed for future use by a gentleman who considers that he is a finer judge of your meaning than you are yourself.

So far, so good. But we are instinctively led hence to the consideration of a different, yet allied, question—as to the frequent habit, on the part of narrators, from one cause or another, of positively tampering with the text of a saying, and falsifying the sense.

For it is by no means with non-essentials only that your special artist deals, or even with minor accessories alone. He holds his licence to extend to the finding you a new hero—one, possibly, who could never, in his most prophetic mood, have ventured to imagine himself in such a situation or in such company.

Sometimes it happens that in a comparatively late chap-book we detect a *rifaccimento* of an ancient legend.

At Glasgow appeared a small roughly printed tract in 1700, with the title of *The New Wife of Beath*, in which we are desired to believe that the text is "Much better Reformed, Enlarged, and Corrected, than it was formerly in the old uncorrect Copy"; and we are farther told that there is "the Addition of many other Things." The preface adds that the " Papal or Heretical " matter in the former copy has been omitted in this second edition, leaving nothing to offend the wise and judicious, "not being taken up into a literal Sense, but be way of Allegory and Mystical, which thus may edifie."

We have here, in point of fact, the story and adventures of Chaucer's Wife of Bath subsequently to her dissolution; and we learn how, after a strange series of vicissitudes, including a visit to his majesty the Devil, who declines to take her in, our heroine finally propitiates Christ by a profession of faith, and is placed among the elect. It is a grotesque tissue of piety and blasphemy, presumably adapted to the Protestant ritual and taste by an anonymous son of the Kirk.

What the reformer suppressed we can only conjecture, since the anterior impression, with the Popish leaven in it, has not fallen under our eyes. In lieu of the Saviour, the Virgin was, perhaps, made the central figure, with the general costume

of the piece to correspond. What he
added it is easier to judge; for, looking at the archaic narrative of "the
Countryman who got into heaven by his
pleading," we perceive that *The New Wife
of Bath* is an amplification of the idea
and scheme; and where the original
middle-age story-teller was content with
the ordeal of the Apostles and the First
Person of the Trinity, his presbyterian
follower thought it necessary to make the
lady run the gauntlet of all the patriarchs
and prophets, and even of our first parents,
all of whom she triumphantly vanquishes,
the concluding parley being with Christ
Himself, who is made to come out on
hearing the disturbance, and is overcome
by her argumentative eloquence and con-
fiding humility.

With the portentous absurdity of the
whole notion, both in its succincter and
more enlarged shape, we need not occupy
ourselves. I merely adduced the circumstance as one of the numerous phases of
my subject; for I presume that no one
will seriously question its title to a place
in the semi-jocular category.

Nothing is truer than the passage in Horace :—

"Multa renascentur, quæ jam cecidere . . . "

In the mediæval story of the Man with Wooden Legs, who succeeds in persuading a stranger that his apparent loss was a positive advantage and blessing, there is a property of permanence ; for, as recently as 1885, a boat was capsized, and the only one who escaped was buoyed up by his artificial limb. This was a recommendation overlooked by the early *conteur*, anxious as he was to exhibit the unsuspected superiority of a substructure not prone to casualties, and not only renewable at pleasure, but useful as fuel when discarded from active service.

CHAPTER VIII.

THE SAME SUBJECT CONTINUED—THE ANECDOTE-MONGER.

THE sophistication of anecdotes is undertaken for the sake of constructing fresh material for the entertainment of the general reader without resorting to original sources. It is of course a process which is confined, as a rule, to popular literature, and to literature only; yet I remember having once seen at an auction a large portrait of Charles II., where, without any becoming regard to the costume, a head of Charles I. was painted in, because the Martyred monarch was dearer to connoisseurs than the Merry one.

The writers of the life of Charles Lamb have gone nearly as far by telling a story, in one version of which Benjamin Jonson figures, and in the other Dr. Johnson, as the personage quoted by Lamb. It was a case in which either would serve the turn; and variety pleases.

The statement of Malone about the elder Richardson sounds the keynote to the present argument. It became part of Richardson's business to collect gossip about his contemporaries and others— in other words, he procured the outlines, and filled in the background and colour, if they were wanting, so far as he judged them requisite for the immediate purpose. He was one of many. Aubrey, Chetwood, Oldys, Walpole, and Malone himself, did much the same. Chetwood is wholly untrustworthy. Aubrey is to be accepted with many grains of allowance. But Oldys, Walpole and Malone were unusually accurate and scrupulous, and took pains to ascertain the truth, or not to set down, at any rate, what they knew to be the reverse.

Valuable as the information and traits preserved by Walpole and Malone must always remain, neither looked much below the surface, or took the trouble to scrutinise very closely the stories which reached their ears,—although we have seen, just above, that the latter, at all events, took true measurement of Richardson.

In the use of made-up tales or gossip, it was doubtless considered that the original outlines were of insufficient interest and dramatic completeness; and we are presented accordingly with a finished scene or conversation built out of a mere meagre skeleton. Like the first sketch of a picture which the artist makes in the fields or on the water, the professional adept in another way obtains his rough material at the club or the dinner-table, and takes it home with him to finish *pro bono publico.*

A curious glimpse of what may be described as preliminary rumination and subsequent cookery is afforded by Malone in what he says about the celebrated Lord Chesterfield :—

"The late Lord Chesterfield's *bons mots* were all studied.   Dr. Warren, who attended him for some months before his death, told me that he had always one ready for him each visit, but never gave him a second on the same day."

Chesterfield's utterances, in other words, were second-hand impromptus—clever things which occur to one after the event, to be brought adroitly in next time. They resemble the speech which the man makes to himself on his way home, but which he should have delivered at the meeting or the banquet.

There are producible specimens, not only of the *radix*, which an artificer elaborates to suit his purposes, but of the converse—where the length of the original saying has been regarded as prolix, and has been shorn of its ample proportions, till it becomes a *mot* or an epigram. Every one has heard, for instance, of the capital observation of Horne Tooke, in reply to somebody who had stated in his hearing that the law was open to all men : " And so is the London Tavern ! "   But the more correct version of this matter appears to be one which is given in *Joe Miller*, 1832, No. 947 :—

" John Horne Tooke's opinion upon the subject of law was admirable. 'Law,' he said, ' ought to be, not a luxury for the rich, but a remedy to be easily, cheaply, and speedily obtained by the poor.' A person observed to him, ' How excellent are the English laws, because they are impartial, and our courts of justice are open to all persons without distinction!' 'And so,' said Tooke, 'is the London Tavern to such as can afford to pay for their entertainment.'"

Here we have an illustration of the imperfect manner in which a presentment in miniature conveys the sense of the speaker. It is by no means *multum in parvo*. Tooke laid down the principle which Brougham subsequently carried into effect, but which proved a virtual dead letter—the County Court machinery, which was to have brought home justice at a low rate to every man's door, but which, in point of fact, has been, from beginning to end, nothing but a sham and a juggle.

There is no story within my knowledge which indicates so clearly and amusingly one of the sources of corruption in the present branch of literature as the following :—

"A gentleman had purchased a jest-book, from which having selected a few tolerable stories, he related one of them, stating every circumstance as having actually happened to himself. His youngest son, a boy about nine years of age, who had occasionally got hold of the volume, sat with evident marks of impatience until his father had concluded, when he jumped up and bawled, 'That's in the book! that's in the book!'"

Now, of course it does not require much calculation to arrive at an idea of the peculiar susceptibility of jocular and anecdotal matter to arbitrary treatment at the hands of every comer. It is truly the poet's *mutato nomine de te.*

There are instances, again, where the text of a jest has a certain aspect of verisimilitude, yet where the peruser is apt on reflection, I think, to conclude that the cook has done his part. Let me illustrate this by a citation:—

"Two men, who had not seen one another for a great while, meeting by chance, one asked the other how he did. He replied, he was not very well, and had been married since he saw him: 'That's good news, indeed,' said he. 'Nay, not such good news, neither,' replied the other; 'for I married a shrew.' 'That was bad,' said the friend. 'Not so bad, neither; for I had two

thousand pounds with her.' 'That's well again,'
said the other. ' Not so well, neither,' said the
man ; 'for I laid it out in sheep, and they all
died of the rot.' 'That was hard, indeed,' says
his friend. 'Not so hard,' says the husband; 'for
I sold the skins for more than the sheep cost.'
' That made you amends,' said the other. ' Not
so much amends, neither ; for I laid out my
money in a house, and it was burnt.' ' That
was a great loss, indeed.' ' Nay, not so great
a loss, neither ; for my wife was burnt in it.' "

A capital anecdote, assuredly ; but the cue
is too sustained for a casual encounter.
It has the air of a hint taken and worked
humorously out.

As there are cases in which matters of
fact are edited *ad hoc*, so does it occasionally happen that a joke is invented to
suit certain given conditions. The name
of a person or place, coupled with some
flexible incident, suggests to an ingenious mind an *ex post facto* happy phrase
or figure, as we see in the commonly
accepted tradition of the actor, Andrew
Cherry, who informed a manager that he
had been bitten by him once, and that
he was resolved he should not make *two
bites of A. Cherry*.

The story of Diogenes and Alexander, where the former asks the king as a favour to stand from between him and the sun, is obviously a literary evolution from the accredited character of the so-called cynic; and the same may be predicated of that where Diogenes flings away the cup on seeing some one drink water from his conjoined hands. The office of biographer, from the dearth of material and stock-in-trade, had already become merged in those of inventor and romancist.

I have elsewhere taken occasion to suggest that the philosopher's so-called tub was some Hellenic pleasantry at the expense of a, no doubt, very humble and contracted dwelling. So we are accustomed to speak of a man living in a box or a crib.

The *dits* with which we are so liberally regaled about exalted personages and crowned heads, are interesting in their way, and here and there may have come down to us pretty nearly as they left the mouths of the reputed authors—as, for example, the annexed :—

"The town of Chartres was besieged by
Henry IV. of France, and capitulated. The
magistrate of the town, on giving up the keys,
addressed his Majesty: 'This town belongs to
your highness by divine law, and by human
law.' 'And by *cannon* law,' replied the king."

The only difficulty is, that *cannon law*
is not the phrase which the speaker would
have used. An English translator has for
once improved his original.

I have stated that the same conditions are
apt from time to time to produce identical
trains of thought. A little trait of the
famous founder of the Bourbon dynasty
in France is on exactly parallel lines with
an actual incident which occurred within
our personal knowledge, and might have
done so within that of a thousand others.
The rank of one of those concerned in
the original anecdote communicates to it,
however, an additional zest. It is said
that, on one occasion, as Henry IV. was
leaning out of window, a fellow about the
palace, mistaking him for an intimate,
slapped him behind. The king turned
round sharply, and the other, in a terrible
fright, stammered out that he thought it

was So-and-so—Jacques or Jean. "Well,"
returned Henry, good-naturedly, "if it
had been, you need not have hit so hard."
An involuntary gravitation to a certain
portion of our frame seems to be a universal and immemorial instinct of human
nature. The truth to say, this choice
morceau has been attributed to Sully as
well as to his royal master.

But too many sayings are either vamped
up and utterly worthless, or are laid
before us in a shape which arises from
sheer ignorance of the costume of the
subject, like the ridiculous descriptions
which occur in the *Bravo of Venice* and
other melodramatic romances. To any
one who is conversant to a fair extent
with the strict and stern *régime* under
the old French monarchy, what can be
more absurd and self-convicting than the
subjoined relation?—

" An honest dragoon, in the service of Louis XIV.,
having caught a man in his house, after some
words told him he would let him escape that
time ; but if ever he found him there again, he
would throw him out of the window. Notwithstanding this terrible threat, in a few days he
caught the spark there again, and was as good

as his word. Sensible that what he had done
would soon be known, he posted to court, and
throwing himself at the king's feet, implored
His Majesty's pardon. The king asked what his
offence was; on which the soldier told him how
he had been injured. 'Well, well,' said the king,
laughing, 'I readily forgive you; for, considering
the provocation, I think you were much in the
right to throw *his hat* out of the window.' 'Yes,
please your Majesty,' said the man; 'but then
his head was in it.' 'Was it?' replied the king:
'well, my word is passed.' "

There was scarcely a court in Europe
with which such an incident could have
been less happily associated; and it is
almost difficult to call to mind any constitutional system, except perhaps that of
the first Napoleon or our own Charles II.,
where such a *tête-à-tête*, so to say, could
have taken place.

Nearly the whole stock which exists
up and down the market of Irish bulls,
Sawniana, gasconades, gaulardisms, and
Mrs. Partingtoniana, has submitted to
the churn. A pattern is produced; and
any given or desired number of impres-
sions may be had to order—no two alike
exactly, and no two very different.

Which was the absolute *jocus princeps* about the Scotch, it is probably at this time impossible to discover; but it is obvious that they are all grafted on one parent stem, and scarcely yield a second moral. The entire assemblage forms a satirical exposure of the alleged parsimonious egotism of the nation. *Ex uno disce omnes :—*

"A Scotch pedestrian, attacked by three highwaymen, defended himself with great courage and obstinacy, but was at length overpowered and his pockets rifled. The robbers expected, from the extraordinary resistance they had experienced, to lay their hands on some rich booty, but were not a little surprised to discover that the whole treasure which the sturdy Caledonian had been defending at the hazard of his life, consisted of no more than a crooked sixpence. 'The deuce is in him,' said one of the rogues; 'if he had had eighteenpence, I suppose he would have killed the whole of us.' "

And it is the same with another group, to which I have lately adverted:—

" 'Soldiers must be fearfully dishonest,' says Mrs. Partington, 'as it seems to be a nightly occurrence for a sentry to be relieved of his watch.'"

Mrs. Partington was nothing more than a lay-figure, on which the ingenious could pass off the *jeu de mot*, which begins to form an element in the *facetiæ* of the seventeenth century. She was a convenient personification, like her successors Mrs. Gamp and Mrs. Brown.

CHAPTER IX.

The Marred Anecdote—Gaulardisms
—M. Goussaut—The Retort and
the Pun—"Maloniana"—Metrical
Adaptations — Second-hand Facetiæ—Parallel Versions.

 SINGULAR *lusus artis* is the
marred anecdote, of which
the most familiar specimen
is the threadbare story of Goldsmith
and the stale greens. But this was a
very old Joe, and seems to have been
first narrated in connection with a couple
of scholars, of whom one laughing at the
other because his garment was too short,
his companion remarked that it would be
long enough before he got another. The
next person whom he met became the
recipient of a version of the matter
immaterially varied, yet so as to give the

death-blow to the witticism. "Jack," quoth he, "I've just heard such a capital joke." "What was it?" "Why, I told Tom that his coat was too short, and he answered that it would be *a long time* before he got another." "Well, I don't see anything in that." "Ah! well," returned the first, "it seemed a very good joke when he made it."

Nearer, however, to Goldsmith's day a very similar pleasantry used to be current about Archbishop Herring when he was at college. Herring, having fallen into a ditch near St. John's, a wag, passing by, called out, "There, Herring, you are in a fine pickle now!" A Johnian, overhearing this, went back to his college, and was asked by some of his friends what made him so merry. "Oh," says he, "I never met with such a good story before. Herring of Jesus fell into the ditch, and an acquaintance said, as he lay sprawling, 'There, Herring, you are in a fine *condition* now.'" "Well," observed some one, "where is the wit in that?" "Nay," replied the first, "I am sure it was an excellent thing when I heard it."

Here, in good faith, was a crassitude which Joe Miller himself would have hardly surpassed in his most Bœotian and opaque moments.

The Gaulardism, borrowing its name from a certain Sieur de Gaulard, who was remarkable for the negation of everything savouring of intelligence, strikes one as of an analogous complexion to this jocular *gaucherie*; and both are intimately allied to the Gothamite drolleries and ineptitudes, of which the most ancient types have very probably and very naturally disappeared by escaping registration. The gaulardisms and their analogues pursue a uniform vein :—

"The Sieur Gaulard, being told by somebody that the Dean of Alençon was dead, said, 'Don't believe it; for, if it were so, I should have heard from him, as he keeps no secrets from me.'"

"A person, seeing a great heap of stones, said to a friend how much he would like to have them at home. 'How so?' demanded the other. 'Why,' said he, 'then I would build a good handsome brick wall round my house with them.'"

The mantle of Gaulard must have descended on the President Goussaut, who, if the anecdotes about him are to be credited, must have adorned his lofty official position. The rest are as by sample exhibited :—

" Monsieur Goussaut, President of the Chamber of Accompts, was celebrated for stupidity. One day standing behind a player at piquet, who did not know him, the player throwing a foolish card, exclaimed, 'I am a mere Goussaut!' The president, enraged at finding his name used as a proverb, said, 'You are a fool.' 'True,' said the other, without ever looking back, 'that is just what I meant to say.' "

Had Goussaut been an English, instead of a French, name, we might have looked upon it as an inadvertent felicity.

Of course these merriments have their equivalents or survivals in the later life and literature; and I may adduce as a specimen the question raised in some company as to the age of Lord Chesterfield, when one of the party suggested that his lordship must be older than was generally supposed, as he would be at least one-and-twenty when he signed the bond which was forged by Dr. Dodd!

Then, once more, there is Mrs. Malaprop, the celebrated *persona* in Sheridan's *Rivals*, who shares with her creator the honour of having said many things for which neither has any actual responsibility. That so familiar aphorism, "Comparisons are odorous," is in a play printed more than a century before Sheridan was swaddled.

In other words, the gaulardism and Malapropism are of all time, just as the intellectual abortions which produce them are. An inadvertence which may be thought to merit classification among gaulardisms, is recorded of a German writer (F. von Raumer) upon England as it was, or seemed to him to be, in 1835, where he speaks of becoming acquainted with the famous Vicar of Wakefield, and describes his gooseberry wine as quite answering to the description of it given in the book !

It is very far from being generally apprehended, indeed, how plentiful and how varied this description of *gaucherie* always has been and still remains. Two instances, separated by a wide interval of time, and entirely distinct in their character, occur to me. In 1615 an anonymous personage reproduced a tract which Robert Greene, the dramatist, published in 1592, under a new title and with an original preface, purporting to be by Greene, in which he refers to works belonging to a date long posterior to his decease.

My second illustration is from another field and from modern life. Mr. Alma Tadema exhibits a picture representing a room in ancient Pompeii, with all the supposed coeval appurtenances; and among these we recognise patinated bronze vases, the property, not of the Pompeian, but of the R. A.

This may be as appropriate an opportunity as I shall have of noticing an analogous type of solecism. In the farce of *High Life Below Stairs* one of the characters inquires who was the author of *Shakespear*, to which a second responds, *Kolley Kibber*. We are here face to face with a piece of small wit, which belongs to the same family as that where surprise is expressed by some sapient individual at the literary activity of Mr. Finis and

7

M. Tome ; or where the foolish Duke of Gloucester envied the good fortune of that rich fellow Co., who seemed to be a partner in so many firms.

I once saw a copy of Thomas May's translation of Lucan's *Pharsalia*, on the fly-leaf of which some simpleton had written, " Ben Jonson, from Thomas May," in order to lead to the supposition, of course, that the book had been presented by one poet to the other. This was a sort of compromise between a jest and a fraud; but an equally ludicrous inconsistency may be found in *Joe Miller's Jests*, 1832, No. 1107, where the familiar anecdote about Randolph being identified by Jonson at the Devil Tavern is given ; and the dramatist, when Randolph had delivered his extempore rhyme about John Bo-peep, is made to exclaim : "*By Jasus*, I believe this is my son Randolph !" and we are gravely informed by the editor that *By Jasus !* was Jonson's " usual oath."

But the complexion of the story, as a whole, is fictitious ; and while I do not for a moment believe that the verse is a contemporary *impromptu*, I am strongly sceptical as to its claim to the character even of a contemporary production. There is no ground for accrediting the poet with the degree of poverty presumable from the description of his clothes and his need of a trifling gratuity; and the very texture of the lines is apocryphal. Besides, the narrator first makes us understand that Randolph was unknown to Jonson and the rest of the company, and then alleges their identification of him from a specimen of poetry which could have furnished no clue whatever to the improviser.

I have dwelt on this point because the biographical scrap, so far from standing alone or being a rare type, is a member of an exceedingly numerous family, and the stricture has a common application to it and its congeners.

The Retort and the Pun, and indeed the entire *genus* of succincter jests, are least prone to editorial treatment. But, on the other hand, there are two classes which, from their nature, have a peculiar and an inherent liability to sophistication —namely, the *Epigram* and the *Story* ;

and in fact the very structure of these
ought to be, as a general rule, a sufficient
indication and evidence of their artificial
development.   The droll and amusing
tales in the old English jest-books have
been obviously woven into a narrative
shape by the original recipient of the
particulars, or by some one else more
experienced in the science of literary
cuisine.   The inimitable account of John
Adroyns, who, after performing on some
provincial stage the part of his Satanic
majesty, walked home in his theatrical
garb, and met with a complication of
mishaps, is an excellent specimen of the
professed jocular compilation by a third
person, as distinguished from a piece
of humour delivered to us exactly or
approximately in the terms which the
actor or actors employed.   So long as a
pleasantry presents itself to notice with
honest credentials, there is no ground for
complaint and no source of difficulty ;
but it is where an anecdote is introduced
under fictitious colours, that the critical
inquirer is apt to feel, if not embarrass-
ment, at least annoyance.

I shall transcribe one illustration of this kind of cross-bred offspring from *Maloniana :*—

" Few classical quotations have ever been more neatly applied than the following. Mr. Burke had been speaking in the House of Commons for some time, and paused. He soon proceeded, and some time afterwards paused again, so long (which with him is very uncommon) that Sir William Bagot thought he had done, and got up to speak. 'Sir' (said Mr. B.), 'I have not finished.' Sir W. B. made an apology, and said, ' As the hon. gentleman had spoken a long time, and had paused unusually long also, he imagined that he had concluded, but he found he was mistaken. Some allowance, however, he hoped, would be made for him as a *country* gentleman, for—

' Rusticus expectat dum defluat amnis ; at ille
Labitur et labetur in omne volubilis ævum.'"

If the process by which the passage from the poet, " so neatly applied," was, subsequently to the event, spliced to it, is not apparent to the reader, I confess that it is so to myself; and few things are less probable than the pronunciation of such an *impromptu* under such conditions. Yet we find Malone, a man of the world and a sagacious critic, setting down the passage in undisturbed credulity and absolute good faith as a fact within his knowledge and as a spontaneous performance in its integrity. It may seem very remarkable that its superficial unlikelihood should not have struck him; but it is the case that entertaining gossip or laughable traits concerning celebrated people usually pass unchallenged, even when a slight scrutiny would suffice to expose their spuriousness either in whole or in part; and it must be remembered that the bulk of our *Ana* have come to us through channels infinitely more open to corrupting agencies and less discriminating than Malone. But the Jest, in its many varieties, is indulgently regarded, whether by the general public, which takes the matter as proven, or by the literary fraternity itself, for whom it serves as a pleasant relaxation from severer studies.

As it is with the Story, so also it fares with the Epigrammatic *bon-mot* or facetious notion thrown into the metrical form. There is a tolerably familiar one, which carries plainly enough on its front, when we approach the subject in an inquiring temper, the traces of its parentage :—

> " A fisherman one morn display'd
>   Upon the Steine his net ;
> Corinna could not promenade,
>   And 'gan to fume and fret.
>
> " The fisher cried, Give o'er the spleen,
>   We both are in one line :
> You spread your net upon the Steine,
>   Why may not I spread mine ?
>
> " Two of a trade can ne'er agree,
>   'Tis that which makes you sore :
> I fish for flat fish in the sea,
>   And you upon the shore."

The frequenters of Brighton fifty years ago would have been familiar with the scene portrayed in these lines, which might be founded on an actual incident or a possible one. The stanzas were, of course, the composition of a wit of the time, and bring before us a glimpse of London-super-mare, before it had parted with all the pleasant characteristics of a Sussex fishing village—when the fisherman could still come up Pool Valley, and lay his nets to dry on what is now an ornamental square !

It is now time to turn to another aspect of this many-sided and, so to speak, ramified subject, and to consider a different phase of the vicissitudes and metamorphoses which this branch of literature not only has undergone, but preserves a constant tendency to undergo. It is the invaluable art of attiring the fresh hero or favourite in the disused habiliments of his predecessors. It affords a signal exemplification of the strange and unexpected fortunes which may attend an adventure or a witticism, as well as of the surprising diversity of uses to which a capable artificer may apply a single suit of motley. We are looking at the genealogical side of the question, the heraldic point of view.

No. 67 of the *Hundred Merry Tales* (1526) treats "of the Scholar of Oxford that proved by sophistry two chickens three." In the Jests of Scogin we similarly encounter "How Jack by sophistry would make of two eggs three."

It is the identical invention lamely repeated, and a jest-book of the eighteenth
century reproduces it once more as an
episode in the life of the Merry Monarch,
where he, Nell Gwynne, and the Duchess
of Portsmouth are the actors, and the
Duchess is made the sufferer.

Again, No. 57 of *Merry Tales and
Quick Answers* discourses " of him that
would give a song for his dinner," reminding us of the popular farce, *No
Song, no Supper.* Let us set before the
reader the version, as it stands in the
volume just quoted, side by side with
a second which is better known. The
parallel is curious ; and I confess that
I am sceptical as to the later text being
more than a literary adaptation after
Jonson's time. If it was a veritable
coincidence, it was an extraordinary
one :—

"There came a fel-
owe on a tyme in to a
tauerne, and called for
meate. So, whan he
had well dyned, the
tauerner came to reken

" Ben Jonson, owing
a landlord some money,
kept away from his
house. The vintner,
meeting him by chance,
asked him for what

and to haue his money, to whom the felowe sayde, he had no money, but I wyll, quod he, contente you with songes. Naye, quod the tauerner, I nede no songes, I must haue money. Whye, quod the felowe, if I synge a songe to your pleasure, will ye nat than be contente? Yes, quod the tauerner. So he began, and songe thre or foure balades, and asked if he were pleased? No, sayde the tauerner. Than he opened his pourse, and beganne to synge thus:

" ' Whan you haue dyned
   make no delaye,
  But paye your oste,
   and go your waye.'

Dothe this songe please you, quod he? Yes, marye, said the tauerner, this pleaseth me well. Than, as couenant was (quod the

was owing to him; but at the same time told him, that if he would come to his house, and answer him four questions, he would forgive him the debt. To this proposal Ben very readily assented, and at the time appointed waited upon the landlord, who produced a bottle of wine, and then put to him these questions: 'First, What pleases God? Secondly, What pleases the devil? Thirdly, What best pleases the world? And lastly, What best pleases me?' 'Well,' says Ben, directly:

" 'God is best pleased when
   man forsakes his sin;
  The devil's best pleased
   when men persist
   therein;
  The world's best pleased
   when you do draw
   good wine;
  And you 'll be best
   pleased when I pay
   for mine.

felowe), ye be paide for your vitaile. And so he departed, and wente his waye."

"The vintner was so well pleased with this impromptu that he gave Ben a receipt in full for his debt, and treated him with a bottle into the bargain."

The details, it will be at once observed, are slightly varied ; but the germ is the same, and the truth appears to be, that a copy of the *Merry Tales* had fallen in Jonson's way, and that he wished to reproduce a drollery which tickled his fancy, and more or less suited his case.

To the same group may be thought to appertain Old Merrythought's song in the *Knight of the Burning Pestle* :—

"For Jillian of Berry she dwells on a hill,
And she hath good beer and ale to sell;
And of good fellows she thinks no ill,
And thither will we go now, now, now,
And thither will we go now.

"And when you have made a little stay,
You need not ask what is to pay,
But kiss your hostess and go your way,
And thither will we go now, now, now,
And thither will we go now."

It may seem to some unkind to disturb
this and other such traditions about distinguished persons; but the blame rests
elsewhere—with the bookseller or author,
who thought fit to propagate these fictions
and *variæ lectiones*; and the restitution of
literary property to its legitimate owners
is among the functions and obligations
of the antiquary.

It was natural for the old booksellers
to draw into their service, in offering a
popular volume to the public, some
more or less magnetic name, which might
play the part of foster-parent to the
jocular collections of an obscure literary
adventurer; but it seems incredible that
any reader or editor should have been
found so wanting in perception as to set
seriously down to Archibald Armstrong
a jest-book and a tract, which passed
current as his at the time of their original
appearance. *Archy's Jests* and *Archy's
Dream* were palpably the productions of
two professional writers, who followed the
common practice of utilising the capital
resident in a departed celebrity.

The rejoinder of Frederic the Great

to Dr. Franklin, when he sought his aid
in establishing freedom in America, to
the effect that he was born a prince, had
become a king, and would never do anything to ruin his own trade, is so far
entitled to the priority over a somewhat
similar trait preserved of Joseph II. of
Germany, "Je suis par métier royaliste,
Monsieur," that Frederic preceded Joseph
in order of time.

The majority of our books of *facetiæ*
contain, however, a reasonable percentage
of matter special to themselves ; the un-
acknowledged recourse to other authori-
ties is only an incidental form of trans-
gression ; and the cases of wholesale
piracy, the extent of the series considered, are not numerically important.
The recommittal to the press of forgotten
miscellanies, with a mere change in the
title or the hero, is almost countable on
the fingers.

Some allowance is to be made, as I
have said, for the intuitive recurrence
of the same idea, moreover ; as where,
in *Scogin's Jests*, one of the stories—
"How the Scholar said that Tom Miller

of Oseney was Jacob's father"—is the original of the joke enunciated with a probable unconsciousness of plagiarism or anticipation by the Christy Minstrels; and, again, as where the account of the gruff old gentleman and the boy Sheridan is forestalled in that highly succulent collection brought out under the auspices of Jack of Dover.

In the latter, a physician and a boy enter into conversation; and when the boy has, as we should say, chaffed his senior pretty freely, the doctor testily observes: "Thou art a rare child for thy wit; but I fear thou wilt prove like a summer apple, soon ripe, soon rotten; thou art so full of wit now, that I fear thou wilt have little when thou art old." "Then," said the boy, "I gather by your words that you had a good wit when you were young!" The students of *Sheridaniana* will recognise a familiar acquaintance here in a strange dress.

CHAPTER X.

BUT it must not be supposed
that those who have interested
themselves in the manufac-
ture of these agreeable diversions made
any rule of waiting for the objects of
appropriation to grow old. The account
of Dr. Parr mistaking his saturated wig,
as it dried at the fire, for *rothe gothe*, was
equally narrated and believed of his contemporary Dr. Farmer; and that about
Bishop Watson and the Old Cock at
Windermere is nothing more than a re-
issue, with a change in the bill, of the

Duke of Cumberland and the Original
Old Grey Ass. It demanded in neither
case the possession of archæological insight to detect the double paternity; for
the two versions and the two men were
living nearly abreast.

Where a certain type is before the world
as a model, it seldom fails to multiply
itself with trivial variations. Take, for
example, three articles from sources dated
between 1640 and 1790; the same thing,
too, is recorded of Sydney Smith :—

"'That fellow,' said Cyrano de Bergerac to a friend, 'is always in one's way, and always insolent. The dog is conscious that he is so fat that it would take an honest man more than a day to give him a thorough beating.'"

"A man being rallied by Louis XIV. on his bulk, which the King told him had increased from want of exercise, 'Ah, sir,' said he, 'what would your Majesty have me do? I have already walked three times round the Duc D'Aumont this morning.'"

"A man was asked by his friend when he last saw his jolly comrade —— ? 'Oh,' said he, 'I called on him yesterday at his lodgings, and there I found him sitting all round a table by himself.'"

The affinity between these is unmistakable. The same train of thought may produce the same fruit with an absolute freedom from indebtedness. It is a rather interesting problem, of which the solution will, perhaps, never be forthcoming. A second illustration is admissible, shewing the same process at work at a different angle :—

EIGHTEENTH CENTURY.	NINETEENTH CENTURY.
"Sheridan told his son that he thought it was high time for him to take a wife. '*Whose* wife shall I take, sir?' was the inquiry."	"When Sydney Smith's physician (Abernethy) told him that he ought to take exercise on an empty stomach, he inquired, 'upon whose?'"[1]

It is not in the least degree a ground for astonishment, that *jeux d'esprit* appertaining to old times have descended to our own in a decomposed or mutilated condition, when we find such fugitive trifles connected with men, who were all but our contemporaries, already parting with the bloom of the mint. Two of

[1] There can be no doubt that the faulty or varying versions of stories of modern origin are often ascribable to the neglect of immediate registration, and the subsequent oral or written repetition from memory.

the biographers of Charles Lamb offer to public consideration simultaneously a *mot* from his lips, in terms beginning to be fairly devious, but which, when a few more years have run out, will by possibility have ceased to be recognisable by the author. *Ecce !*

"MR. PROCTER.	"MR. FITZGERALD.
"An old lady, fond of her dissenting minister, wearied Lamb by the length of his praises. 'I speak, because I *know* him well,' said she. 'Well, I don't,' replied Lamb, 'I don't; but damn him at a venture.'"	"A lady once bored him a good deal. 'Such a charming man! I know him! Bless him! I know him!' To her Charles, wearied with repetition of this encomium, — 'Well, I don't; but *damn him at a hazard.*'"

The two records are approximately similar ; yet the discrepancies are rather serious, taking into calculation the nearness of Lamb to us and to the literary gentlemen who have made it their business to chronicle his good sayings. The editorial setting has somewhat overlaid the mounted jewel.

None of our Shakespearian students

has hitherto addressed himself to the special task of tracing to their sources the few pieces of gossip about the poet, save, perhaps, the deer-stealing episode. The *Richard III. and William the Conqueror* story, in which Burbadge and Shakespear are made to figure, is recorded by Manningham in his Elizabethan Diary, and no earlier analogue has fallen in my way. The scandal about Davenant is another item of the same class, which we are almost ashamed to find ourselves cherishing, even though it be, as it were, *formâ pauperis*, from sheer lack of better matter. It seems lamentable that, while the anecdote-hunter was on the trail, he did not appropriate, for the benefit, in struction and delight of every intelligent individual coming after him, some particulars of Shakespear's private and literary life, once so easy of access, now so irretrievably lost ! How many thousand biographies of all kinds of nonentities might not be exchanged for an account of Shakespear by an educated contemporary !

Malone refers to the foundation of the Literary Club and to a little episode about

Garrick and Johnson in connection with
that event :—

"Not very long after the institution of the
Club," he says, "Sir J. Reynolds was speaking
of it to Garrick. 'I like it much,' says he; 'I
think I'll be of you.' When Sir J. Reynolds
mentioned this to Dr. Johnson, he was much
displeased at the actor's conceit. 'He'll be of
us!' says Johnson; 'how does he know we will
permit him? The first duke in England has no
right to hold such language.' However, when
Garrick was regularly proposed, some time afterwards, Johnson warmly supported him . . ."

"On the former part of this story,"
adds Malone, "it probably was that Sir
John Hawkins grounded his account that
Garrick never was of the Literary Club,
and that Johnson said he never ought
to be of it. And thus it is that this
stupid biographer, and the more flippant
and malicious Mrs. Piozzi, have mis-
coloured and misrepresented every anecdote that they have pretended to tell of
Dr. Johnson.'"

The reader does not require to have
the story of Raleigh, questioning the cause
of some disturbance under his window
in the Tower, retold. Tradition is too

indispensable to be cut away, yet too
treacherous to believe without misgiving
or without some convergence of proof.
I have been turning over the pages of
the *Hundred Merry Tales* and the *Merry
Tales and Quick Answers* in quest of a
few specimens of what might be adduced
and regarded as original matter, and how
thin is my harvest! Yet, onerous as are
the obligations even of these ancient collections, the debt, it must be owned, is
of a character and degree differing very
essentially from that under which their
successors lie to them again. For where
there is loan or trespass, it is almost
exclusively from obscure foreign sources
unknown to the generality of readers, and
betwixt we certainly get many an enjoyable
bit of downright home-grown merriment
or rascality. Among these I may be permitted to commend to attention the tales
"Of the miller that stole the nuts of the
tailor, that stole a sheep," a piece of mas-
terly structure, "Of the fat woman that
sold fruit," "Of the courtier that bad the
boy hold his horse," "Of him that healed
frantic men," which is cited both by Sir

John Harington and Robert Burton, and
" Of the two young men that rode to
Walsingham." These, and a dozen more
scattered over the two books, have an
insular air, although they may not be
without their continental analogues. They
look as if they had first seen the light
on British ground, circumscribed by the
waves which wash our cliffs ; but anyhow
they in their turn formed part of the
general stock-in-trade, out of which a
totally distinct class of men from More
and Heywood here, and Erasmus abroad,
carried on for ever and for ever the
business of amusing a not very fastidious
and not very critical constituency.

The gratification at meeting once in
a way with an anecdote in its pure and
pristine state, is like the feeling when one
secures an old picture with which the
cleaner has not tampered, or a coin exempt
from *tooling* and corrosion.

There is, comparatively speaking, a
handsome residuum after all deductions
of genuine English *Ana* in the two Tudor
books, in which I elsewhere intimated a
suspicion that Sir Thomas More and John

Heywood had a hand ; and there are also
a few exceptions to the almost universal
rule, that the old jest is by nature in-
tractable—that is to say, archaic—not
merely in language and orthography, but
in temper, structure and blood. If one
arranges in parallel columns the original
text of the greater number, or rather the
mass, of these relations, and a modern
version, the alteration is merely external.
The costume and tone in both are alike
obsolete. Conspicuous and valuable illustrations of the contrary occur, however,
in No. 7 and No. 48 of the *Hundred
Merry Tales*, and No. 14 of the companion book. Nothing can be less dependent upon time than the account " Of
the friar that told the three children's
fortunes " : if it is out of date, Boccaccio
and Chaucer are ; and in that other, " Of
the chaplain, that said Our Lady's matins
a-bed," there is a piquancy worthy of
Sydney Smith.

Items are frequently inserted in jest-
books by the editors or collectors without the most distant suspicion of their
veritable origin and character ; and it

also happens to this sort of literary composition, as it is known to do to engravings, that they exist in various stages of recension and in various degrees of divergence from their *prima stamina.*

The process of affiliation, as I venture to call it, is necessarily cognate to that of corruption. The emigrant tale, whether from one part of the world, or from one book, to another, is bound to undergo a change of garb or one in the *dramatis personæ.* I shall proceed to exemplify this :—

"In a village of Picardy, after a long sickness, a farmer's wife fell into a lethargy. Her husband was willing, good man, to believe her out of pain; and so, according to the custom of that country, she was wrapped in a sheet and carried out to be buried. But, as ill luck would have it, the bearers carried her so near a hedge, that the thorns pierced the sheet and waked the woman from her trance. Some years after, she died in reality; and as the funeral passed along, the husband would every now and then call out, 'Not too near the hedge, not too near the hedge, neighbours.'"

This is not the version of the incident usually current, for that substitutes a hearse for the bearers, a coffin for the sheet, and a tree against which the carriage was run, overturning the supposed corpse, and causing her to revive.

But, first removing this latter superincumbent *stratum*, or ignoring it, let us examine the particulars, as I have just printed them. Have we not before us a mode of sepulture unknown to Western Europe in the conveyance of the woman to her grave simply enveloped in a cloth ? That is, of course, Mohammedan, and is precisely the method pursued in India by the disciples of that creed at the present moment.

One doubt begets another ; and the presence of a hedge appears to betray the revising touch of one of my own countrymen, as it is so infinitely more characteristic of the narrow gorge-like lanes of rural England than of the route which a similar procession would be likely to have followed on the other side of the Channel.

So it seems as if we had before us an Oriental tradition or invention, first introduced into French literature at a period when the languages and learning of the East were more cultivated in that country than among ourselves, and finally Anglicised, first with the hedge, and secondly with the bearers and the coffin, as novel and improving ingredients.

But the whimsical anecdote of Martin Elginbrod perhaps even more strikingly exhibits the longevity of certain tales or apologues, the curious phases through which they pass, and the need of approaching them, for their full appreciation, in a critical temper. Here we have, for instance, what appears superficially to be a mere piece of grotesque incongruity and irreverence on the part of a sober-minded Caledonian, who figures as the composer of his own epitaph :—

> "Here lie I, Martin Elginbrod :
> Have mercy on my saul, Lord God !
> As I wad do, were I Lord God,
> And ye were Martin Elginbrod,"

which constitutes at first sight a libel on parity of reasoning and the law of proportion, and at the same time a piece of speculative licence unusual among the disciples of the Kirk; but on closer scrutiny the lines present to us perhaps the most successful attempt ever made in the way of a revival. The inscription itself is probably an immediate transfer from the Dutch, in which language it occurs *mutato nomine*; but the idea was mooted three thousand years ago in the sacred books of the Hindoos. In its modern dress the notion is, of course, a pure extravagance; but such an inversion of established doctrine and belief in the Vedas becomes less startling, when we reflect that the theological system there developed is of a less sublime and immutable type than our own, and does not so entirely forbid this hypothetical or imaginative change of relationship.

These transmitted relics of Elginbrod and of the coffin seem to shew in a pronounced manner how a sentiment or idea which is implanted in our very nature is susceptible of reproduction and adaptation without an obvious betrayal of its original appurtenance to former ages and other creeds.

The story in *Merry Tales and Quick Answers* of the woman who lifted up her nether garments to conceal her head has the air of having voyaged from Egypt or some other Oriental country, where it would be the instinct of any female, even at the present day, to do exactly the same thing at all risks, the exposure of the face being contrary to religious canons. The author of the *English-woman in Egypt* relates an anecdote to this point.

Shakespear's witty notion of the black flea on Bardolph's red nose, to which the modern anecdote of Sambo and the mosquito appears to be under obligations, is circumscribed by the introduction of the doctrine of eternal punishment as to date. I have thought that the same idea might have occurred to any one philosophically contemplating the dark specks in a blazing coal fire.

The *fons et origo* of witticisms is often very difficult to reach—nearly as much so as the source of the Nile. In one of his Letters, Charles Lamb quotes, as a good saying of Coleridge, the joke, " That summer has set in with its usual severity." The curious point is that Byron had made the same facetious

remark just before ; but Lamb and he
belonged to different sets. It matters
little, however, for Walpole had anticipated them both ; and the present *mot*
appears to be the Joseph Miller query,
" When did you ever see such a winter?"
To which a wag retorts, " Last summer."

An almost exact parallel to this is found
in the comparison by Coleridge of the
pure and undefilable mind of Charles
Lamb to " moonshine which shines on
a dunghill, and takes no pollution." In
the *Life of St. Agnes*, by Daniel Pratt,
1677, the saint is made to liken God to
the *sun*, shining on a dunghill without
being defiled ; and in the *Lives of the
Philosophers*, by Diogenes Laertius, Diogenes the Cynic is made to employ the
same figure of speech. Whence did *he*
borrow it ?

Another singular case of affiliation
presents itself to our notice in the sermon
preached before thieves by Parson Hobart,
to whom his uncustomary congregation,
after he had done what they required to
their satisfaction, returned the money
whereof they had relieved him on the

road, adding six shillings and eightpence
as a fee for the discourse. This occurs
in a tract of the time of Charles I.,
which bears the following quaint title :—
" Forced Divinity, Or Two Sermons
preached by the Compulsion of two Sorts
of Sinners, viz. Drunkards & Thieves.
The one by Certain Ale-Bibbers, who
having heard a Minister teach much
against Drinking, afterwards met with
him, and compelled him to make a
Sermon upon one word. The second,
by a Crew of Thieves, who after they
had robbed a Minister, forced him to
make a Sermon in Praise of their Profession, and when he had done, Returned
his Money, and Six Shillings Eightpence
for his Sermon."

Now, this very tale about Parson Hobart
is in an early MS. printed in *Reliquiæ
Antiquæ*, and is in fact a mere resuscita-
tion for the nonce, which is made additionally manifest from the sum named
as the gratuity—six and eightpence or
a noble, a species of currency which had
gone out of use in the seventeenth
century ; so that, had we not known that

the story was far older than it purports
to be in the tract above quoted, there
is a kind of internal clue to its superior
antiquity—one considerable enough, but
insignificant when we measure it against
the distance between Martin Elginbrod
and the Vedas.

Into certain works of fiction, not
professedly or specifically jocular, the
humorous side or element has been
unwittingly introduced by the authors in
connection with the treatment of their
topics; and in one or two cases at least
it is so much so, that the whole production amounts to little better than an
elaborate and tedious jest. The *Bravo
of Venice*, by Monk Lewis, to which I
allude elsewhere, is, by way of example,
from first to last a solemn absurdity. It
purports to narrate a series of extraordinary adventures in the city by an
Italian prince in disguise; and Lewis,
who seems to have been exhaustively
ignorant of the institutions, habits, and
costume of the Republic, paints with
the utmost nonchalance a succession of
scenes in which his hero is the central

figure, and not one of which could have possibly occurred under the strict and vigilant oligarchical government ruling there supreme—an administrative machinery so thorough and so omnipresent, that no one could raise a finger or utter a sound unobserved and unreported. Yet in this serio-comic romance the Bravo performs a variety of thrilling and marvellous exploits, bespeaking the existence of an executive of the loosest type, with an *éclat* and an impunity possible only in a melodramatic performance or a South American democracy. He even represents to us, in one of his theatrical tableaux, the lovely Rosabella of Corfu, the Doge's own niece, seated alone in an arbour attached to some public gardens, and as rescued from assassination by the Bravo, who is discovered at the last moment, not by the Venetian officials, but his own act, to be somebody totally different from the character which he had originally assumed. It is not too much to say that on that soil such a mystery would not have outlived one round of the clock.

CHAPTER XI.

The Ballad and the Nursery Rhyme—
Philosophical Side of the Question
—"Jack the Giant-killer."

THE normal jest-book limits itself to stories of the ordinary jocular cast relative to incidents either of the current or past time. Neither the compiler nor the peruser, as a rule, concerns himself with any other aspect of the question than the utility of the volume as a source of immediate amusement. The existence of a philosophical side to the matter remains unsuspected.

But I have already tried to demonstrate that this is an intrinsically valuable body of literary material, with which we have to deal, and that it lurks

9

in a wide variety of forms. I have illustrated some of them; but there are yet others—namely, the BALLAD and the NURSERY-RHYME.

The taste for burlesque in composition set in at a very early period, as will become evident from a perusal of these pages, and may be regarded to some extent as a counter-movement to the practice of *moralising* secular productions which were thought to be of an irreligious tendency, and to be susceptible of a different kind of treatment, like the *New Nutbrown Maid upon the Passion of Christ*, the *Court of Venus moralized*, the *Gude and Godly Ballets* of our Northern neighbours, and *Come over the bourne, Bessy, to me*. Of the last, singularly enough, there are two parodies— one political, in which Queen Elizabeth is the heroine, and the other allegorical, in which the speaker is Christ, and Bessy, Mankind. But the original was of an amatory complexion.

Certainly, on the whole, one of the ballads in a printed collection of the reign of James I., entitled *Deuteromelia*,

1609, affords the most powerful and diverting example of the manner in which our own ancestors handled the present class of undertaking, as well as a proof of the appreciation of the ludicrous by the readers of those days. It is an extremely clever production, which I am tempted to transfer hither entire :—

> "Martin said to his man,
>   Fie! man, fie!
> Oh, Martin said to his man,
>   Who's the fool now?
> Martin said to his man,
> Fill thou the cup, and I the can;
> Thou hast well drunken, man:
>   Who's the fool now?
>
> "I see a sheep shearing corn,
>   Fie! man, fie!
> I see a sheep shearing corn;
>   Who's the fool now?
> I see a sheep shearing corn,
> And a cuckoo blow his horn;
> Thou hast well drunken, man:
>   Who's the fool, now?
>
> "I see a man in the moon,
>   Fie! man, fie!
> I see a man in the moon,
>   Who's the fool now?

I see a man in the moon,
Clouting of St. Peter's shoon.
Thou hast well drunken, man :
  Who's the fool now ?

"I see a hare chase a hound,
  Fie ! man, fie !
I see a hare chase a hound,
  Who's the fool now ?
I see a hare chase a hound,
Twenty mile above the ground ;
Thou hast well drunken, man :
  Who's the fool now ?

"I see a goose ring a hog,
  Fie ! man, fie !
I see a goose ring a hog,
  Who's the fool now ?
I see a goose ring a hog,
And a snail that bit a dog ;
Thou hast well drunken, man :
  Who's the fool now ?

"I see a mouse catch the cat,
  Fie ! man, fie !
I see a mouse catch the cat,
  Who's the fool now ?
I see a mouse catch the cat,
And the cheese to eat the rat ;
Thou hast well drunken, man :
  Who's the fool now ?"

Of course, it is easy to condemn such

lines as foolish or old-fashioned; but
there is nothing else exactly like them
in our literature, and they shew the
relish for humorous travesty on the part
of the English public in the sixteenth
century. They obviously do not respond
to the later and existing notion of what
a Jest is; but they may be regarded as
forming an antique type of the songs
introduced into the modern extravaganza
and burletta, and they fall within the
present category as representing one of
the shapes which facetious literature
assumed, before the *Ana* existed as a
distinct branch of research and source
of entertainment.

In ballad-lore there are many other relics
of a playful or comic turn, which do not
involve any jocular sense or plot, as the
Wedding of the Frog and the Mouse,
the *Wedding of the Fly,* and some of the
familiar pieces in the *Drolleries* by the
wits of the court of the Stuarts. A
playwright once offered a MS. farce to
a manager, and assured him, by way of
recommendation, that it was no laughing
matter. That was a bull; but a story or

an idea may be funny without fulfilling
the conditions of a jest ; and, paradoxi-
cal as it may appear, there are cases
where jests may be fairly admissible as
such without offering a direct provocation to laughter. I refer to the nature,
not to the quality, of the performance.

In the Nursery Rhymes of this
country, of which Mr. Halliwell-Phillipps
has made an excellent collection, there
is a good deal that seems suggestive
beyond the mere jingle of the verse or
even the oddity of the subject. The
editor himself, indeed, has indicated
numerous instances in which an historical
or archaic interest underlies the surface ;
and it is curious that this is usually latent.
The rhymes upon the oldest themes, such
as King Arthur, Robin Hood, and Tom
Thumb, are by no means the most ancient
compositions.

A little quatrain :—

> " Three wise men of Gotham,
>   Went to sea in a bowl;
>   And if the bowl had been stronger,
>   My song would have been longer "—

is a remarkable survival of the familiar

traditions about the Gothamites, and may be commended for its elliptical succinctness. It is within the bounds of possibility that the author of *Jack a Nory* had this before him as a model. The conception and structure are so similar. How much is told in a few words! The brush of a Turner could not have wrought a result so instantaneous and impressive. The writer, a true poet, shrinks from harrowing details, and tells the tale with a simplicity almost Druidical.

The next is of a varying texture:—

> "Hush thee, my babby,
>   Lie still with thy daddy
>   Thy mammy has gone to the mill,
>   To grind thee some wheat,
>   To make thee some meat,
>   And so, my dear babby, lie still."

We here find ourselves thrown back on a period when each district or village had its common mill; and all the racy stories about the jolly miller and his golden thumb, and his tricksome tolldish, and his amours with the fair sex, come into our heads. How dull and pithless some of our earliest books of facetiæ would have been without the miller and his brother-rogue, the priest! The drollest anecdotes are of one or the other of these two. How many homes must have been rendered wretched by the visits of the goodwives to Dusty-poll and their intrigues with the sly rascal; and if the husband went in lieu of his spouse, the priest was at hand, in the grey of the morning even, to take his place. It was Scylla or Charybdis — between the devil and the deep sea.

The nursery epic of *Jack the Giant-killer*, of which we do not possess any archaic text or form, displays in a sort of allegory the protest of the people against the oppression of their feudal lords. This tyranny survived perhaps longest in such regions as Cornwall and Wales, or the Cornish and Welsh were unusually intolerant of it. The two-headed giant, whom Jack exterminates in Wales, may be taken to be a land-lord or seigneur of a more than commonly malignant type.

Here is a final sample of a relic

ostensibly recent in origin, yet on closer examination with the crust of antiquity collected upon it :—

> " A cow and a calf,
>   An ox and a half,
> Forty good shillings and three ;
>   Is that not enough tocher
>   For a shoemaker's daughter,
> A bonny lass with a black e'e ? "

Agricultural statistics would shew one, no doubt, how long ago—how many kings' and queens' reigns ago—it was that a cow and a calf could be had for £2 3s. That is the key to the date of the rhyme, in fact ; for the difference in the value of money merely goes to establish that the personage who espoused the shoemaker's daughter had no reason to complain of the fortune given with her. But the pecuniary equivalent has ceased to be quoted these two centuries or so ; and the lines thus carry within themselves a proof of their appurtenance by birthright to a prior era.

There is another class of tale, comprised in the Nursery Series, which resembles a new dwelling built out of

old materials.   It is the one beginning,—

" There was an old man, who lived in a wood,
        As you may plainly see ;
    He said he would do as much work in a day
        As his wife could do in three."

The idea was used by the author of a
farce called *Domestic Economy*, in which
that eminent comedian, Mr. Edward
Wright, formerly signalised his genius ;
but the true original, both germ and
substance, is a jocular invention of at
least the fifteenth century, and what we
see before us is an elaborate amplification, reminding us of the difference
between a country and the map of it
drawn to scale, or between a tragedy
in five acts and the slender plot.

The evidence which the Nursery
Rhyme so often supplies of having once
belonged to a remote literature and
society, is not directly relevant to the
present subject.   But it seemed to enter
into my scheme to draw attention to
this among the many repertories in which
the all-pervading JEST is to be found in

new attire—to the hidden properties
which may reside in popular trifles,
and to the strange mutations which a
certain section of folk-lore has undergone in the process of transmission
to us. A *jeu d'esprit* of Ben Jonson,
which was not impossibly an affiliation
in his case, leaves its last echo, as
it were, in a witticism still more
degrees below proof,—*videlicet*, the
following :—

> " I'll sing you a song,
>   Though not very long,
>   Yet I think it as pretty as any ;
>   Put your hand in your purse,
>   You 'll never be worse,
>   And give the poor singer a penny."

Here the soul of the humour is, that
the preamble is the text—the house is
all portico, or like the shop-frontage in
a pantomime.

But occasionally items present themselves which are jests without any attempt
at disguise, and appear more properly,
indeed, to belong to Joe Miller's Miscellany than to Aunt Louisa's. Is this not
a retort pure and simple, thrown into

metrical form, rather than a little poem
for little masters ?—

> " The man in the wilderness asked me,
>   How many strawberries grew in the sea ?
>   I answered him, as I thought good,
>   As many red herrings as grew in the wood."

This cross-bred effusion, with its share
of epigrammatic character, is traced back-
ward to the last century but one ; it is
in reality of unascertained age ; it bears
no chronological stamp ; it is precisely
a *mot*, which might have been uttered
to-day or five hundred years ago.   It
alludes to the wild berry mentioned by
Shakespear, with a probable stretch of
poetic licence, as cultivated in the Bishop
of Ely's garden near Holborn in the
fifteenth century ; it may have been so
in Gerarde the botanist's time, a hundred
years after.   But the small sylvan variety
must be of great antiquity.

In the entire body of nursery literature,
however, the humorous element seldom
exceeds a sportive under-meaning ; for
the fully developed joke it is an uncon-
genial atmosphere ; and the interesting

constituency to which it addresses itself
would not be capable of penetrating the
drift of a thorough-paced *Joe.* Where
such features occur in a collection of
children's rhymes, they are to be treated
as waifs and strays, which have smuggled
themselves in under some disguise, and
require an experienced eye to single them
out. All that can be said is, that the
book is not much the better for them,
and would not be much the worse
without them. They have a bizarre air.
They are apt to strike a jarring chord.

CHAPTER XII.

CONTINENTAL INFLUENCE—THE " ANA "
—THE " CONVIVIAL DISCOURSES "—
WHIMSICAL INVENTIONS—SHAKESPEAR
JEST - BOOKS — CHANGE IN PUBLIC
TASTE.

HE influence of Erasmus, More,
and a few of their illustrious
contemporaries, at the revival
of learning, contributed a good deal to
make extracts from the ancient writers
popular among the limited reading
community, and to draw the literary
thought of the sixteenth century into
harmony for a time with that of the
later Roman era. This renders it less
difficult to understand why the first
makers of jest-books thought fit to
intersperse their collections with choice
passages from Plutarch and the rest.
They appealed to a current taste and
a sure market. The great Rotterdam wit
and philosopher appreciated sallies and

strokes of humour which, in a modern English club or at a modern dining table, would scarcely stir a muscle ; and he almost killed himself with laughing over the *Epistolæ Obscurorum Virorum*, in which it is hard to discern where the peculiar piquancy ever lay. It is certainly fair to recollect that we cannot transfer ourselves to the intellectual air in which Erasmus and his friends lived. We are unable to look at things of this kind from their seeing-point. What does not strike us as very droll might strike a Dutchman three centuries since very naturally and very forcibly as being so. We know, of course, how much depends in these cases on a turn of phrase, a trick of pronunciation, or any other subsidiary element ; and so far as the *Epistolæ* are concerned, it must be borne in mind that such a travesty was then a novel experiment in literature, and was apt enough to tickle the fancy of a man who was at once so good a classical scholar and modern Latinist as Erasmus.

The taste for selections of Anecdotes,

historical, literary, and miscellaneous, must appear more intelligible; and long before anything on the same scale was attempted in England, or even in Southern Europe, the Basle press found a sufficient demand for this sort of light, gossiping literature, freely salted with *gaillardise*, to exhaust at least four editions of a work three volumes strong —namely, the *Convivial Discourses*, a Latin compilation, which lays down the lines on which our own early books of the same class were modelled, and which profess to have been gleaned over the dinner-table, from the private conversation of friends, from ordinary hearsay, and out of books. It is observable that the second and third volumes signify— which the first does not—the special value of the miscellany *Omnibus verarum virtutum studiosis*; which, as many of the examples and anecdotes given are conspicuously licentious, must be taken in a deterrent sense.

But the ingredients of these evidently popular *Discourses* bespeak the prevalent tolerance in the country of their birth, and on the Continent generally, for a robust freedom of tone and expression parallel with that which made jest-books cast in a similar mould acceptable to the early Englishman—not, perhaps, so much for the virtues which they inculcated, as for the pervading vein of comicality and diversion from severer reading. The old-fashioned school of humour, which the Continental *literati* may be considered to have established, long survived its founders, and was still in a tolerably flourishing condition when Shakespear wrote. It did not die thoroughly out till the end of the last century; but the Georgian period in England saw the rise of a different taste and style, which largely resulted from constitutional and social changes in our system, and which gradually elbowed out of favour the archaic jocular spirit and the multitudinous *Ana.*

To that revolution I shall have an opportunity of adverting presently; and I must now call attention to the collection of Old English Jest-Books which edited in 1864.

10

This was a fairly representative *Corpus*, embracing the best productions of the class, in all its varieties, during the sixteenth and seventeenth centuries. It was advertised by the publishers as *Shakespear Jest-Books*, because Shakespear mentions one of them casually in one of his dramas; but the volumes seem to connect themselves with him in a more direct and sympathetic manner, when we examine them side by side with his own comic episodes and creations, and see how the old-world, quaint fun of the plays is in unison with that of the books.

Both are emanations from the time; and they occupy a middle station between the Dutch school and our own. Shakespear and his fellow-dramatists placed upon the stage familiar types, employing familiar language; and the setters-out of jest-books and they had, commercially speaking, one mission—that of putting forward only what use had stamped current.

There was still one remaining class of jest, which was once a very favourite form of pleasantry, and which, if it survives at

all, survives under an altogether changed
aspect. This is the Whimsical Invention,
such as—

*The Merry Tales of the Mad Men of
Gotham.*

The Sackful of News.

*Jack of Dover his Quest of Inquiry for
the Veriest Fool in Christendom.*

*Pasquil's Jests, with Mother Bunch's
Merriments and a Brown Dozen of
Gulls.*

One of the Puritan writers denounces
the first article on our list as one of
the "witless devices" of the Elizabethan
age; and he is very near the truth. Of
course, they are far older than that
reign, and are mentioned in the *Hundred
Merry Tales;* nor does the small book
which holds them, contain them all, or
represent the original date of their introduction to the public notice in a printed
shape. They belong to the family of
Noodledoms, Gaulardisms, and Gasconades, which seems to have enjoyed such
general acceptance for a great length of
time both in England and on the Continent; and while they are no doubt

prodigiously silly, I am quite serious in
my assurance, that I should be very sorry
not to have them, and that I would liefer
spare many literary memorials than this
and the other Fooleries, with which they
are on terms of relationship.   Any one
who chooses to refer to *Old English
Jest-Books*, 1864, will understand my idio-
syncracy, for there, at a much earlier
period of my life, I took considerable
pains to illustrate both their former
acceptability and their to-day's use.   I
have seen them described as ineptitudes;
but that was by such as lacked critical
insight, and left the mineral treasure un-
gotten.   A superficial examination will
not do; the divining rod must be applied.
We must break the surface, and within
are wonders surpassing those of the cave
of Aladdin.

I would not have it to be supposed
that these Gothamite and other drolleries
are altogether destitute of point or legi-
bility; but for my present purpose I
have no space to linger over them, and
hardly any occasion, as they offer no
original types.   They are, for the most

part, *bis cocta*—an unconscious homage to preceding authors, with the subsidiary features varied for the nonce. Even *Mother Bunch* is nothing more than Elinor Rumming revived with certain additions and melodramatic embellishments ; and *Jack of Dover* offers little that is novel to our consideration beyond the conception of a jury of penniless poets—reaching, so far as it is possible to make out, the abnormal number of twenty-eight—as a vehicle for a series of thin, vamped-up jokes, in the majority of which we easily identify old friends, and not improved by a change of clothes.

The present rarity of the bulk of this species of literature, and even disappearance in not a few cases of works or editions which must once have existed, are to be explained indeed by the insatiable hunger for novelty in external presentment and the neglect of discarded favourites quite as much as by the other more usual incidence of popularity.

When we cross over from an investigation of the older literature in order to make a general survey of the modern

school, it is like the migration to a
different climate. Something resembling
an organic revolution has occurred in
this sphere of action and ingenuity.
New literary and theatrical agencies have
been in operation. Great political con-
vulsions and the overthrow of dynasties
have made their secondary effects sensible.
The Georges have turned everything
upside down. Grandfather's jest-book is
equally out of date with his opinions
and his costume. Joe Miller has won
a victory more signal and more enduring
than Blenheim. He is the jocular laureate
of the new Hanoverian time, and of all
time to come. His book, if he only
knew it, is to see as many editions as
the *Pilgrim's Progress*, and to have as
many readers as the Bible. He is to
become in his way a colossus—a cyclo-
pædia in himself.

What more could the most aspiring
solicit or desire?

Soberly speaking, the appearance of
*Joe Miller's Jests, or the Wit's Vade-
mecum*, under fortuitous circumstances in
the time of George II., marked the new

era in this description of industry, and
was an English Hegira.

It was as if the jest-books of all prior
epochs had been gathered unexceptionally
up, and burned by the common hang-
man, to let the British community start
afresh. So broad was the line of de-
marcation between the Old *régime* and
the New; and it is not difficult to see
that this truly marvellous change is an
evolution from novel phases and develop-
ments of social life, and was just what
was to be anticipated. In this special
way, perhaps, a more complete alteration
had taken place since the Tudor period
than has taken place between the last
century and the present one; or, in other
words, in the last hundred and fifty years.
We cannot believe that an ordinary reader
of Henry VIII.'s days would have had
any relish or value for the fun of the
earlier half of the eighteenth century;
but an ordinary reader of the present
time perfectly appreciates the anecdotes
and humour—not exactly of the primitive
lean *fasciculus* to which *Joe Miller* was at
the outset limited, but of the wits who

flourished under Walpole and side by side with Pope.

This group of men, authors, actors, dandies, and *bons viveurs*—is the true lineal ancestry of Sheridan and Matthews, Sydney Smith and Jerrold; and, *mutatis mutandis*, the form, temper, and tone of the school have suffered no material variation, since its first rise into an immortal existence under the auspices of Miller within the genial precinct of Clare Market.

It is upward of two decades since I launched the so-called " Shakespear Jest-Books"; and, looking at them to-day, I cannot help saying that I see in them a means supplied to the inquirer of forming a comparative estimate between the ancient school and the early English on the one hand, and the modern English on the other. The volumes form a selection of types from 1526 to 1639, and embrace within their limits almost every variety of jocular invention. Even in the miscellany which passed under the name of *Tarlton's Jests* there had been commencing symptoms of a change of fashion and requirement ; and in Taylor the Water Poet's budget of *facetiæ*, which he christened his *Wit and Mirth*, 1629, we perceive that the revolution has reached a farther stage. The strokes of fun, which delighted the contemporary readers of the *Hundred Merry Tales*, still preserved their place ; but with them are mingled anecdotes more redolent and characteristic of the Stuart period, preparing us for those still later and still grosser publications which marked the reign of the second Charles.

The *Hundred Merry Tales*, with which the series naturally and properly opens, sets the example of plagiarism by adopting stories from still earlier sources ; but the obligations of the book to ready-made or convertible material are relatively slight, and the best portions, including the inimitable account of the " Miller that stole the nuts of the tailor that stole a sheep," and the dramatic story of the Maltman of Colebrook, seem, so far as one has the means of judging, to be founded on actual incidents.

The tales bear constant and unmistakable testimony of having been composed

by some one who possessed a keen sense
of humour and a hearty relish for the
ludicrous ; that they were from the hand
of a literary man and a scholar of no
mean ability, is not to be reasonably
doubted ; and if we were informed on
credible authority that some of them
offered to us the fruits of the leisure of
even so distinguished a public character
as Sir Thomas More, we should receive
the ascription without misgiving, and feel
that there were among his graver works
some which we could better spare.

Not only the relationship subsisting
between More and the Rastells, but the
peculiar tone and cast of the tales, long
since induced me to speculate on the
possible concern of the author of *Utopia*
in their production ; and every one is
aware that More was noted for his
pleasant and facetious conversation, although it may not be so generally familiar
that he signalised himself as a versifier,
and as the writer of the droll tale of the
tipstaff who tried to pass himself off as a
friar.   Yet of course there is not a tittle
of direct evidence in this direction ; and,

again, it is impossible to avoid the per-
suasion that not indeed the mere father-
lessness of the work or absence of a name
on the title, but the complete silence of
the biographers and literary critics of and
after the time on this point, tell against
the idea. On the other hand, the official
position of More, in an even greater
measure than his religious tenets as a
strict upholder of the Romish hierarchy,
made the open association of his name
with an enterprise so uncomplimentary
to the Catholic priesthood eminently
impolitic and inexpedient either as actual
part of the title or as mere matter of
hearsay.

But if it was not More himself, it was
a person of congenial temperament, of
whose identity he must have had some
shrewd hint from the printer, and who had
no taste for literary notoriety or for the
ordinary bookseller's garnish in the way
of seductive forefronts. For a title-page
more laconic and uncommercial was
probably never bestowed on a book of
the kind.

CHAPTER XIII.

The "Hundred Merry Tales"—The Authorship Discussed.

THERE is, however, a second hypothesis bearing on the parentage of the *Tales*. In the *Interlude of the Four Elements*, which came from the same press a few years before, there is the following passage :—

Sensual Appetite. Canst get my master a dish of quails,
Small birds, swallows, or wagtails ?
They be light of digestion.
    Taverner. Light of digestion ?   For what reason ?
    Sen. For physic putteth this reason thereto,
Because those birds fly to and fro,
And be continual moving.
    Ta. Then know I a lighter meat than that.

Sen. I pray thee, tell me what ?
Ta. If ye will needs know in short and brief,
It is even a woman's tongue,
For that is ever stirring."

Now, the ninth story in the Jest-book,
in the edition of 1526, is "Of him that
said that a woman's tongue was lightest
of digestion"; and we have exactly the
same notion reproduced. Conversely,
the nineteenth story in the *Tales* treats
"Of the four elements, where they should
soon be found"; and here very curiously
an analogous notion about the qualities
of the female tongue discloses itself thus :
"The wind said, 'If ye list to speak with
me, ye shall be sure to have me among
aspen leaves or else in a woman's tongue.'"
Water and fire were to be found in a
woman's eye and in her heart; the earth
alone was stationary and steadfast. And
even in the moral we are told that "by
this tale ye may learn as well the property
of the four elements as the properties of
a woman."

These are rough indications, which must
go for what they are worth. And in
the same way, No. 3 of the *Tales* relates

an adventure in connection with the
performance of a stage-play in Suffolk, in
which the devil was a person of the drama.
Theatrical exhibitions in the provinces
were not of very usual or frequent occurrence in those days. This particular one
is alleged to have taken place in a certain
market town ; but, perhaps to prevent the
possibility of giving offence, the name is
withheld. But the narrative strikes me,
from its minuteness of detail, as emanating
from somebody who was on the spot,
rather than from a secondary source, and
from the pains and skill with which the
plot is elaborated as the composition of
a professional writer. And the question
arises whether the reporter of the two
jests was not also the author of the stage-
play in Suffolk and of the *Interlude of the
Four Elements.*

I submit this suggestively and experi-
mentally, since it appears to me that, next
to More, JOHN HEYWOOD is the most
probable candidate for the honour of
having furnished Rastell with the MS. of
the *Tales* ; and if he did so, we may have
a sort of clue to the authorship of two

dramatic productions not hitherto comprised in the list of his writings.

Nor does the connection of More himself with the *Tales*, even under such circumstances, absolutely fall to the ground, as Heywood and he saw a good deal of each other ; and Gabriel Harvey, Spenser's friend, and an affectionate student of the curious literature of the period, informs us that some of his (Heywood's) epigrams were founded on conceits and devices of More.

There are, nevertheless, clear grounds for regarding this Century of good things as a gathering to which More and Heywood were contributors, rather than as the exclusive property of either of them, or of any one else. For we see, for instance, that in the fortieth story a man so celebrated and even notorious as Skelton, and at the time of the publication of the *Tales* still living, is described as "one Master Skelton, a poet laureate," which seems to argue the presence behind the scenes of an editor not very conversant with contemporary literature or literary history ; and this might be possibly true

of Rastell the printer, but could not be so
of More or of Heywood.

But then, only a little way farther—in
the forty-eighth anecdote—we are con-
fronted with the admirable apologue " Of
the friar that told the three children's
fortunes," where, after declaring to the
horrified mother that of her family one
should be a beggar, a second a thief, and
the third an assassin, he consoles her by
saying that she might make the one who
was to be a beggar *a friar*, the one
who was to be a thief *a lawyer*, and him
who was destined to be a murderer *a
physician.* Here we recognise the touch
and individuality of no ordinary pen, and
discover an additional explanation of the
reluctance which the compiler or contributors felt to couple any names with
the volume. Attacks on the Romish
Church were treated in 1526 with a larger
measure of toleration than heretofore ; but
in this jest three obnoxious callings, including that of More himself, are exposed
to satire.

One drawback to the dramatic completeness of the anecdote is the aspersion

which the Friar Mendicant is made to cast on his own cloth ; and we at the same time cannot avoid discerning a trace of the root of the incident in some *fabliau* composed in far more primitive times than those of the appearance of the first English jest-book. For we are introduced to the wife of a very rich man, standing at the entrance of her husband's dwelling, accompanied by her children, and subsequently with her own hands spreading the repast, of which the friar partakes. The intention was to create a laugh at the cost of the three vocations ; but the *rédacteur* neglected to observe all the conditions necessary to render the hit perfectly true to art.

CHAPTER XIV.

UT there is a second work which, in point of date and character, is sufficiently near to that which we have just quitted to warrant a conclusion that the editor had in its production an eye to the earlier book. Many of the jests in *Merry Tales and Quick Answers*, printed about 1530, resemble those which I have almost convinced myself that Sir Thomas More and John Heywood contributed to the volume from Rastell's press; but, on the whole, the collection is of inferior interest and value, and owes more to foreign and classical sources

There is even here, however, a curious coincidence between the fifty-third story

and a feature in the Interlude before re-
ferred to. In the anecdote the man, who
is not worthy to open the gate to the king,
proposes to fetch *Master Couper* to do
it, while *Tom Couper* is introduced in the
same sort of casual way into the dramatic
performance. Among these tales the
fellow who entertained so humble an
opinion of his worth was a true coeval
type, while he who elsewhere could only
see in his sovereign lord "a man in a
painted garment" was a Radical born out
of his time. Yet both jests bespeak such
a liberality of temper as could enjoy a
laugh at the two pieces of bucolic ignorance alike, which makes our thoughts
return naturally to More.

In indelicacy there is not much to
choose between the two series; but it has
always been a misapprehension to deduce
from the equivocal situations and language,
which go so far to make the marrow of
these popular compilations, a proof of the
tolerance among our ancestors of a freedom
of speech no longer admissible. The
grossness of early English literature is
not displayed, after all, most conspicuously

in jest-books, but in the drama; and we have assuredly nothing which parallels in obscenity the old popular literature of the French.

There is, however, one important consideration to be taken into account when we enter on the study of this class of material, whether prose, poetical or dramatic,—and that is, the social station of the individuals into whose mouths these broad pleasantries are put. Occasionally, no doubt, expressions are ascribed, rightly or wrongly, to men, and even to women, in an exalted rank of life, which seem revolting to modern taste; but, although such traits do not, as a rule, find their way into type, distinguished persons of the present day are capable of a good deal in this direction, and in the last century high-born dames delivered utterances which would certainly be now viewed as extremely improper, without concealment or a consciousness of having said anything unconventional.

The standard of politeness has perhaps been raised, if that of morality has not. We confine ourselves in our vices to the closet, and observe good behaviour in the street, and even, on the whole, at the theatre. But, to return to the more immediate subject, the coarseness and ribaldry which distinguish and season the early jest-books principally emanate from the lower strata of the population—from the folk, in fact—which is no whit superior at this moment to the use and enjoyment of a similar phraseology and a similar description of merriment. Place the carter and the bargeman, the market-woman and the orange-wench, of the reign in which we live, side by side with the analogous characters when the *Hundred Merry Tales* appeared, and see whether in three centuries and a half refinement has made much progress ! *Pares cum paribus.*

I insist on this point a little, because the moral and virtuous ladies and gentle-men of the Victorian era are in the habit of averting their faces from the lamentable depravity of former ages, as if it were some once rampant monster now defunct, and because the change in our manners is vulgarly attributed to the influence of

the Court.   The latter delusion arises
from the common error of mistaking cause
for effect ; the open profligacy of former
reigns is discarded in the same way as
that of our literature and theatre ; the
modus vivendi of the Georges is archæological ; if such doings and sayings are
any longer, they are under the rose.

But it is a pharisaical absurdity to give
out that there is no such matter as low
life upstairs nowadays.   Alas ! it is too
rife ; and, it being so, we have surely no
right to be so very hard on Whitechapel
and the New Cut.   That the general tone
of the British community is higher and
purer proceeds from the influential pre-
ponderance of the middle class ; and
the court, and in general the aristocracy,
conform to the march of civilisation.

Queer stories must be *inter nos*.   Altered
circumstances have rendered it imprac-
ticable to bring them into print or to
introduce them upon the boards.   Be
thankful for small mercies ; but do not,
my dear contemporaries, flatter your-
selves that you are, warp and woof, much
better than those who read on their first

appearance the *Hundred Merry Tales* and the *Merry Tales and Quick Answers*, or that by reading them you would be made much worse!

CHAPTER XV.

FACETIOUS BIOGRAPHIES.

EAVING behind us these two admirable productions, we encounter an interesting group of compilations, which differ essentially from them in structure and treatment. They constitute a sort of family of books, and are of a biographical cast, with an imperfect attempt at chronological sequence. I shall enumerate some of them :—

The Jests of the Widow Edith.
The Merry Tales of Skelton.
The Jests of Scogin.
Tarlton's Jests.
The Merry Conceited Jests of George Peele.
The Pleasant Conceits of Old Hobson.
Dobson's Dry Bobs.

The original motive for associating a particular individual with a publication was obviously the stimulus which his reputation was expected to lend to the sale. The real tie between a facetious miscellany and its god-parent was, in nine cases out of ten, absolutely nominal. In the reputed adventures and pranks of the Widow Edith, Skelton and Scogin, there is the largest share of verisimilitude; but the printed accounts, especially in the case of Scogin, are so long posterior to the epoch at which the heroes flourished, that there was infinite opportunity for laying to their credit any current jokes or tricks of a suitable complexion.

Of the three, the tracts dealing with the poet and the widow leave the impression, on perusal, of being narratives of authentic incidents in a far greater degree than the *Scoginiana*; and some of the anecdotes of Skelton are superlatively funny,—for instance, that which narrates "how the cobbler told Master Skelton it is good sleeping in a whole skin." But it is unfortunately too lengthy for transcription. There is not only a stronger air of probability about the anecdotes which we here find of the parson of Diss than in those which occur of Scogin, but an agreeable exemption from grossness, although it has been surmiscd that both came from the same pen—that of Dr. Andrew Borde, of Pevensey.

Shakespearian readers are familiar with the passage in *Henry IV.*, Part I., Act ii., where Falstaff is discovered asleep behind the arras, and his pockets are turned out, disclosing a tavern account, in which the charge for sack is the principal item, and for bread only a halfpenny is set down; whereupon Prince Hal exclaims to Poins, "O monstrous! but one halfpennyworth of bread to this intolerable deal of sack!" The germ of this passage seems to be in the story relating "how the Welshman did desire Skelton to aid him in his suit to the king for a patent to sell drink"; and another point is that the song "Back and side go bare, go bare," etc., introduced into *Gammer Gurton's Needle*, embodies the same idea.

Chaucer makes his Sumner describe himself as "a man of little sustenance,"

but does not let us hear whether his
predilections were for liquids or solids.

Apart from their dubious personality,
the jests of Scogin have their clear utility
and worth as a picture of archaic social
life ; they furnish glimpses of obsolete
manners and notions with merciless can-
dour, and eclipse almost the entire body
of *Ana* in unrestrained licence of expression.   But, as I have hinted, Scogin is
more or less of a lay-figure, and some of
the achievements for which he enjoys the
credit are of foreign origin.   At least two
of them meet the eye in the " Book which
the Knight of the Tower made for the Use
of His Daughters," printed by Caxton,
and not unknown to Dr. Borde ; and this,
while it may detract from their originality,
is a plea on their behalf, as some of
the borrowed matter, which was thought
fit reading for young ladies by a noble
French author and their parent, is certainly among the less decent portions of
a not very decent volume.

The good knight himself, however, was
part of a world less verbally or outwardly
prudish than ours.   He had only to dip

into the written literature of his time to find plenty of such anecdotes as he introduced into his book, and as have become familiar to us through the collections of *fabliaux*, where numerous examples offer themselves to our view of the identical conditions of ancient domestic life. I shall not attempt to decide whether the moral atmosphere of France in the thirteenth century was better or worse than that which we breathe; but the knight and his family were surrounded by it, and knew no other.

Of the other jest-books falling within the biographical category, the *Jests of George Peele* and the *Conceits of Hobson* are palpable *réchauffés*—warmed-up dishes of stale viands. The same is to be predicated of *Dobson's Dry Bobs*, which claims on the title-page to be a kind of sequel to Scogin.

Tarlton's Jests present the aspect of a tolerably contemporary, if not homogeneous and individual, assortment of witticisms and exploits. They are chiefly redolent of the court and the theatre, the two scenes of his activity and triumphs;

and if all the things which they make him
say or do were not said or done by him,
it is not easy to point out the sources to
which the editor of the original book
went. Tarlton was undoubtedly a man
of rare powers, and his celebrity must
have long outlived him. He died in the
plague-year 1588, before Shakespear came
to settle in London, yet not before the
great dramatist might have seen him and
spoken to him ; and for some time I have
entertained a suspicion that he may be
the Yorick of *Hamlet.*

The *Jests of the Widow Edith, the lying
Widow which still liveth,* is an early Tudor
book (1525), which, though not dissimilar
in its nature from Skelton and Scogin
and the German *Eulenspiegel,* varies dis-
tinctly from them all in being a history in
doggerel rhyme, composed by one of the
dupes of a licentious and unprincipled
adventuress, named Edith, whose strata-
gems and impostures are rehearsed in
this quaint metrical record with graphic
minuteness. The date of the tract—the
first quarter of the sixteenth century—its
popular tenor, and its uniqueness of type,

may together do something to disarm our anger at its literary poverty and its occasional latitude,—although, were not a lady in the question, it is not so offensive as the low buffoonery of Scogin, or as some of the items which found their way into the Tarlton volume.

The relations of Skelton with his parishioners in Norfolk form a curious chapter in the ecclesiastical annals of the reign of Henry VIII. His eminence as a writer and celebrity as a humourist have doubtless contributed to preserve for our edification a tolerable salvage of his sayings and doings while he held preferment in the Church; but it is the circumstance that he was something more than a loose parson which has given such prominence to his irregularities, just as there were, in the time of Shakespear, deer-poachers whose names we have not been enabled to recollect.

The so-called *Merry Tales of Skelton* amount, in reality, to a slight biographical sketch strung together in sectional form. There even appears a sort of attempt at chronological propriety, as they begin prior to his instalment at Diss and close at a point in his life when he was under the displeasure of Wolsey—not for his profligacy of behaviour, but for his vituperative writings against that powerful minister.

As a picture of the manners of the time, without a study and knowledge of which it is obviously futile to try or presume to judge Skelton or anybody else belonging to it, the narrative of the mistress whom the poet kept at his living, his reprehension by the bishop, and the scene in Diss church when (according to the jest-book) he rated his congregation for complaining of him and openly exhibited the child, baffles competition, when one takes into account the relations of the pastor to his flock, the severity of ecclesiastical discipline, and the rebuke which Skelton had suffered immediately before at the hands of his spiritual chief. It is when we contemplate such social phenomena that we become more and more forcibly convinced that the Reformation was not a crusade against immorality, but a political fight between the Church and

State. In the case of Skelton himself, his licentiousness would probably have never involved him in serious trouble had he not chosen to attack Wolsey.

But the entire texture of this small miscellany of humour, scandal and libertinism is cross-woven ; and its serious value is, to my apprehension, greater than its comic. For it not only sheds light on certain points in the career of the singular man with whose name the tales are directly associated, but on the whole surrounding atmosphere.

CHAPTER XVI.

ANALECTA.

T was not till the Greeks and Romans had arrived at an advanced stage of civilisation that scope was afforded to the class of writers of whom we are accustomed to regard Athenæus and Aulus Gellius as typical examples; and somewhat on a similar principle the development of the jest in the more modern acceptation is traceable back only to a certain stage of social order, when a perception of the ridiculous or eccentric was quickened into life by the establishment of an artificial standard among us of politeness and opinion.

Another and distinct section of jest-books consists of what may be treated as the pioneers of the English Ana—collections made by editors from other books

12

and from hearsay among their friends or
in company ; and of these I shall content
myself with adducing as specimens—

1. *Wits, Fits, and Fancies*, by Anthony
Copley, 1595.

2. *Certain Conceits and Jests*, 1614.

3. *Wit and Mirth*, by John Taylor the
Water Poet, 1629.

4. *Conceits, Clinches, Flashes, and Whimzies*, by Robert Chamberlain, 1639.

5. JOE MILLER'S *Jest-Book*, 1739.

A century and ten years elapsed between the publications of Taylor and
Miller ; but the earliest edition of the
latter was barely more than a pamphlet,
and would not be at first sight recognised
by those who are only familiar with the
more recent issues, in which the original
text has been amplified and overlaid, till
the slender proportions of the shilling
book of 1739 are completely effaced.

The copious title of Taylor's performance speaks for itself : " Wit and Mirth,
chargeably collected out of Taverns,
Ordinaries, Inns, Bowling Greens and
Alleys, Alehouses, Tobacco-shops, High-

ways, and Water-passages, made up and
fashioned into Clinches, Bulls, Quirks,
Yerks, Quips, and Jerks." The arrangement closely follows that of *Tarlton's
Jests* and the *Conceits and Jests*; but the
plan is widely dissimilar, since Taylor
has comparatively little to say about
himself, and the work, such as it is, is
his own; whereas Tarlton stood to the
book which carries his name merely in
the relation of sponsor, and the whole
is devoted by the actual editor to him
and his real or putative extravagances.

The self-evident truth is, that Master
Taylor jotted down every smart saying or
racy passage which fell in his way by road
or river, or wherever his professional and
private engagements happened to take
him. He was rather indiscriminate and
not very squeamish; and his budget exhibits wares of all sorts as well as of all
shades of quality and every variety of
character, new and old, original and
borrowed, prose and verse. Yet, taken as
a whole, the farrago has very great general
merit; and we must be content to set what
is dull and dirty, clumsy sophistications

or inferior variants, against the moderate residue of valuable permanent matter, where we get unique touches of contemporary persons or little insights into the thought and habits of the age. The whole, if the author is to be believed, underwent at his ingenious and experienced hands a sort of churning process; and, altogether, it is a book which we lay down, as we do all others of the kind, with an uncertain and dissatisfied sensation.

If I transcribe three samples from the *Wit and Mirth*, it must be with the proviso that no one shall blame me if, on resorting to the work, they do not meet with much more of equal excellence :—

"Master Thomas Coriat (on a time) complained against me to King James, desiring his Majesty that he would cause some heavy punishment to be inflicted upon me for abusing him in writing (as he said I had) ; to whom the King replied, that when the lords of his honourable privy council had leisure, and nothing else to do, then they should hear and determine the differences betwixt Master Coriat the scholar and John Taylor the sculler ; which answer of the King was very acceptable to Master Coriat."

" A soldier upon his march found a horse-shoe
and stuck it at his girdle, when, passing through
a wood, some of the enemy lay in ambush, and
one of them discharged his musket; and the shot
by chance lighted against the fellow's horse-shoe.
'Ha! Ha!' quoth he, 'I perceive that little
armour will serve a man's turn, if it be put on in
the right place!'"

" A chorister, or singing-man, at service in a
cathedral church, was asleep when all his fellows
were singing; which the Dean espying, sent a
boy to him to waken him, and asked him why
he did not sing. He, being suddenly awaked,
prayed the boy to thank Master Dean for his
kind remembrance, and to tell him that he was
as merry as those that did sing."

There is a story about Barkstead, the
poet and actor, which is hardly suitable
for repetition, although it reminds us of
one narrated of St. Louis of France ; and
there is a second of Field the dramatist,
which is not worth quoting. The account
of the drowsy chorister really refers to
Richard Woolner, who belonged in the
early years of Elizabeth to the choir at
Windsor, and whose propensity for som-
nolence was doubtless occasioned or
aggravated by his voracious appetite.
This Richard Woolner was a pleasant

fellow in his intervals of consciousness ;
and in 1567 an account of him and his
oddities, no longer known, appears to
have been printed. Sir John Harington
mentions him in his *Brief View of the
State of the Church.*

CHAPTER XVII.

The Subject continued.

HE taste for these *Analecta* grew with the supply. They proved popular and easy reading, and did not exact much reflection on the part of the peruser or a large amount of literary skill in the compiler. No operation is perhaps simpler than the construction of a book out of a series of paragraphs found at intervals and strung together at random. *Tarlton's Jests* seems to have led the way and set the fashion, and the press has been busy with such *olla podrida* ever since.

Judgment in selection is, of course, the grand postulate in this as in every department of art, and it is precisely there that the workman in all times has fallen short of success ; so that the whole mass of pirated matter, from first to last, is capable of yielding scarcely more than sufficient to fill a volume of fair compass.

For instance, I discern only a single scrap in the *Certain Conceits and Jests,* 1614 :—

"There was a certain fool that always, when the sun shone, would weep, and when the rain rained would laugh ; and his reason was, that sunshine followed rain, but rain sunshine."

So, again, in the *Conceits, Clinches, Flashes, and Whimzies,* of 1639, where the arrangement is similarly in paragraphs, but where at the same time the contents answer better to the title than to the Ana, there are 287 heads, and to discover half a dozen passable illustrations is a task of difficulty. These *bijoux,* which the author, a Lancashire man, carefully garnered up as they struck his own fancy, or fell from the society which he kept, are after the following style :—

"An antiquary," says one, "loves everything (as Dutchmen do cheese) for being mouldy and worm-eaten."

"A simple fellow in gay clothes is like a cinnamon-tree ; the bark is of more worth than the body."

"Another said, a woman was like a piece of old grogram, always fretting."

A few more might be added, not for their wit, but for their casual elucidation of some obsolete word or custom ; but we must not deny the writer the credit of introducing the PUN. Better have been made since ; but, after all, we are here in the days of Charles I. N⁰· 145 inquires why few women loved to eat eggs? *Answer :* Because they cannot endure to bear *the yoke.* A far from brilliant effort spoiled in the wording !

"Why are tailors like woodcocks? *A.* Because they live by their long bills."

Perchance, the best in this indifferent medley is N⁰· 177, which depends on the different meanings of *liber* and *libra* :—

"A rich bookseller wished himself a scholar, and one said to him : 'You are one already, being *doctus in libris.*' 'Nay,' replied the other, I am but *dives in libris.*'"

These classical essays do not suit our climate very well, yet nothing is to be objected to them where, as in the one just cited, they are *pure.* But I strongly dislike hybrids, by which I intend such

a retort as the Oxford Don is alleged to
have made to the youths who hissed him
as he passed—*Laudatur* AB HIS; and the
quotation of a line from the Eclogue of
Virgil, where a lady's dress is torn by a
fiddle, is barely more than a verbal conceit, though incomparably preferable to
the aggravating *all-us jelly-us* of Brother
Crug, which is a mere phonetic abortion.

Whatever verdict may be pronounced
on their successors, as they approach our
own period, it must be said of the assem-
blages of *facetiæ*, made public by former
generations down to the last century, that
they leave us no alternative but this
conclusion—that, with exceedingly few
exceptions, considering the space of time
involved, the genuine, enjoyable, laughable, recallable jest was unknown to
antiquity, and is the offspring of modern
thought and conditions.

Of the *jeux d'esprit* and humour of the
olden days the archaic cast is not merely
in the spelling or in the matter, but it is
in the bone and blood; and just as it
would be idle to imagine that an Englishman of the Tudor epoch could be

converted into a modern Englishman by arraying his person in modern clothes, so it is futile to attempt to draw the jocular literature of passed centuries into harmony with our own by adapting the orthography and language to the prevailing mode.

Save in a few rare cases, where the life of the subject is indestructible, the entire body of old-fashioned wit and wisdom is as exotic as a tropical plant within the Arctic circle.

CHAPTER XVIII.

"JOE MILLER'S JESTS" — HISTORY, CHARACTER, AND SUCCESS OF THE PUBLICATION — JOHN MOTTLEY THE EDITOR.

POSSIBLY it might be more correct to regard *Joe Miller's Jests* as marking a new era in this branch of literature and department of ingenuity than as a work possessing pretensions to rank as a model to succeeding editors of similar collections. I am speaking of the little shilling volume originally issued under the care of John Mottley in 1739, and not of the modern publication which bears the same name, and has little beyond the name in common with it.

Mottley's book appeared just when

the stage and the literary world were
beginning to assume an importance and
to exhibit a development favourable to
the formation of coteries and centres;
and as the conditions and spirit of contemporary life govern so completely the
facetious and satirical speech of an age
or a century, the social and political
changes which accompanied the accession
of the Hanoverian dynasty introduced a
new school of wit among the frequenters
of the theatres, clubs and coffee-houses.
In fact, the popularity and success of
Joe Miller's Jests at the commencement
mainly arose from their association with
a defunct actor and their share, such as
it was, of dramatic flavour. There had
been, and was, an abundance of books
dedicated to a similar object, in the
market; but this particular one was
supposed in some special and mysteri-
ous manner to depict, in the first place,
the hitherto unknown and unsuspected
humorous side of Joe's character, and,
secondly, to embody master-strokes of
other great wits of the day and brother
comedians of Drury. The new Court

and Government of the Georges were to
have their own fresh appointments and
effects throughout, authors and actors
included ; and the light literature of
the time shared the universal influence.
The merriments and drolleries of the
Stuart era were discarded to make room
for a different style of production, of
which Joe Miller happened to be the
first in the field, though by no means
so in order of excellence.

Yet, in spite of the shortcomings of
this famous volume, there remains the
important consideration, that it contained
a certain enduring element in its cast
and tone, and that substantially all those
books which have poured incessantly
from the press since that day follow
the same lines and general principle.
The older collections are archæological
and pre-historic ; the precedent *Ana*
and *Facetiæ* are as saurians to the
ordinary reader ; and Miller and his
humble imitators — the Sheridans, the
Footes, and the Sydney Smiths—shut
out from obervation, so far as the
community at large goes, the jocular

treasures and triumphs of ante-Millerian Britain.

In the last century, among Dr. Johnson and his friends, the Elizabethan and Jacobean literature of all kinds met with limited acceptance and lukewarm admiration; its principal utility and interest were from the point of view of the adapter or plagiarist; and innumerable appeals to public favour presented themselves in forms with which the reader and the buyer had more immediate touch and sympathy. The rarest and most precious editions of Shakespear and other writers of his epoch were to be had for a smaller sum than the *Life of Joe Hains*, the *Jests of Polly Peachum*, or any other fugitive performance damp from the printers. Malone tells us that Dr. Johnson could not admire the Duke of Buckingham's *Rehearsal*, and thought that "it had not wit enough to keep it sweet, nor sufficient vitality to preserve it from putrefaction"—a truly Johnsonian pleonasm, but also a key to the sentiment of the generation to which Johnson belonged, and of which he was decidedly

a more than average representative.   But
here we have a case where the writer
could hardly have been viewed as obsolete or illegible in the same manner
and sense as the older playwrights; but
Johnson nevertheless — and   thousands
would have concurred with him—did
not relish the humour of a piece produced only some twenty years before he
was born.   The context and atmosphere
were   wanting;   and if such was the
feeling about the   *Rehearsal*—of which
the merit has recommended it, by-the-
bye, to a recent editor—what prospect of
survival could exist for the swarm of
popular cates with which the English
press had teemed from the reign of
Henry VIII. to the Revolution?

Malone preserves an anecdote which
helps to illustrate the difference between
the old and modern schools tolerably well :

"Mr. Lock, of Norbury Park, well known for
his collection of pictures, statues, etc., was a
natural son.   On his marriage with the daughter
of Lady Schaub, who had been very gallant,
Horace Walpole said very happily, ' Then everybody's daughter is married to nobody's son.' "

The *jeu d'esprit* was reserved for Walpole, though the circumstance on which it was founded had happened often enough before; but in point of fact it was a saying strictly characteristic of the period, and in the author of it we recognise a signally representative type of the latter-day, as contrasted with the old-world, wit.

Walpole, indeed, belonged to the modern school of humourists, which may be said to date back to the era of the Restoration, but which did not, so to speak, attain adult growth till the fuller development of the club and the coffee-house as aids to the theatre in the establishment of new jocular canons and doctrines.

The book called *Joe Miller's Jests* was, both in its inception and its progress, an emanation from the altered state of feeling in regard to such matters. The early editions were, in a literary aspect, wretched enough, and destitute alike of judgment and taste on the part of the compiler. But if the sponsorship of Miller was originally of a nominal and shadowy character, it must be said that, as the volume received from time to time additions, which doubled and trebled its bulk, from an endless variety of fresh sources, the fatherhood of the worthy actor became by degrees absolutely fictitious—a mere *nom de plume*; and it is not too much to allow that, with all its weaknesses, the work in its augmented shape, as the ordinary reader is accustomed to come across it, is a creditable sample of its kind, and will probably yield a better insight into the particular field of inquiry than any other single publication in our language.

Of course, the first impression of 1739 and the current text are so distinct from each other as to have practically little in common between them beyond the name and the tradition. It started by being a strange tissue of deceptive pretences; but it hit the nail on the head; the notion tickled the public fancy; and the title is almost part of the British constitution. The ancient lines have long been obliterated; the pamphlet of seventy pages has swollen into a volume

of five hundred ; and the editor and
publisher are recollected only by the
curious ; while in all literary centres and
among nearly all classes of readers the
man whose name was affixed to the
venture without his consent or knowledge, and whose personal capabilities
in the joking way were below zero,
remains a household word from century
to century, like the superscription over a
venerable house of business of partners
who have been dead and buried these
hundred years, and survive above the
door and on the bill-heads from considerations of expediency.

John Mottley, who strang together
the *editio princeps* of Joe Miller in 1739
for a bookseller, cannot be commended
for the skill and care with which he
executed his task. It is a singular
jumble of anecdotes of all complexions
about persons in various walks of life.
The seventy-two pages were reckoned,
no doubt, dog-cheap at a shilling, under
all the imposing circumstances and seeing
the choice nature of the miscellany,
and the highly distinguished personages

to whose *memorabilia* it strictly limited
its cognisance—*videlicet* and to wit, King
Charles II., Mr. Gun Jones, Sir Richard
Steele, the Duchess of Portsmouth, a
country clergyman, Ben Jonson, Mrs.
C——m, Sir William Davenant, two free-
thinking Authors, a very modest young
gentleman of the County of Tipperary,
Tom Barrett, Lord R., Henry IV. of
France, the Emperor Tiberius, and
others. A richer bill of fare was barely
possible, and it is difficult to understand
why Mottley should not have been proud
to associate himself with such company
and with such a feast of delights, instead
of employing the pseudonymy of Jenkins.
This playful piece of *supercherie*, however, was outdone by the courageous
declaration that the contents were mostly
"transcribed from the mouth" of Joe
himself, and the remainder collected in
his society; for, as a serious matter of
truth, the sole item in the thin octavo,
which the collection makes, really attri-
butable to the then recently deceased
comedian, is of a nature calculated to
inspire us with satisfaction that the title-

page is less veracious than it ought to have been, and almost as much a truant in an opposite direction as was perhaps practicable. The material gathered by Mottley in the first instance was in-different enough surely; but the solitary specimen which he actually furnishes of the facetious vein of his hero must induce everybody to feel thankful that he stopped short there :—

"Joe Miller sitting one day in the window of the Sun Tavern, in Clare Street, a fishwoman and her maid passing by, the woman said, 'Buy my soles, buy my maids!' 'Ah, you wicked old creature!' said honest Joe. 'What! Are you not content to sell your own soul, but you would sell your maid's too?'"

The benevolent forbearance of Mottley was advantageous to the sale of the book confided to his editorship; and the best jest of all was the title and con-ception. To put forward as the author of all good things a poor fellow who could not make a joke, or even see it when it was made by a friend, was an idea as happy as if some speculative genius were to announce a jest-book

by Mr. Spurgeon or the philanthropic Earl
of Shaftesbury.   But the most popular of
preachers or philanthropists would not
have answered the purpose so well at the
moment as a defunct theatrical performer,
equally impervious to humour, but to the
play-going public infinitely more familiar,
not as a wit, nor even as the cause of it
in others, but on purely negative grounds.
A notable piece of triumphant charla-
tanry, as this *Joe Miller* in the first
beginning was, has happened, from a
singular caprice of fortune, to overshoot
the original design and proportions, to
change its fugitive and perishable nature,
and to accommodate itself from time to
time to enlarged and different require-
ments.

The circumstance must be treated as
accidental ; for, looking at the question
on every side, the book has had from
the commencement a host of competitors,
possessing at least equal merit, at least
equally inviting forefronts, and even the
superstitious prestige of the green-room.
But these, one and all, unaccountably
disappeared from the public view ; and

Miller proved the only phœnix, the only sterling coin, the only lasting trade-mark.

Spiller's Jests, Penkethman's, Quin's, nay, Garrick's, were things of a season, the *nugæ canoræ* of their day. Joe witnessed their coming and going; and he is with us yet! He will endure as long as the earth's crust—as long as Shakespear, and longer, perchance, than Milton.

One of the consequences of this huge and matchless renown is that, in the amplified *Vade Mecum for Wits* of Joe the Great, a considerable assortment of comic incidents is enrolled under that talismanic name an age or twain after the date, when all that was soluble of the Miller of Millers had been lifted across from the purlieus of Clare Market to the hospitable shelter of St. Clement's opposite.

CHAPTER XIX.

JEST-BOOKS CONSIDERED AS HISTORICAL
AND LITERARY MATERIAL—THE TWO-
FOLD POINT ILLUSTRATED—LOCALISA-
TION OF STORIES.

HAVING now dealt at reasonable
length with those points of
view which have reference to
the sophistication and affiliation of Jests,
let us proceed to regard this highly
fruitful topic from one or two other
aspects; and firstly I propose to invite
attention to the valuable material which
the writer on old English manners and
institutions may find here ready to his
hand. There is barely a custom or an
idea prevalent among our forefathers
which the vast body of printed *Ana*, and
especially the *Shakespear Jest-Books*, 1864,
do not afford the means of illustrating

and facilities for more clearly compre-
hending. The stories embraced within
the entire range of jocular literature are
so multifarious in their origin and drift,
while they so largely partake of a popular
character, that they richly reimburse our
examination of them, even when, as so
frequently happens, their literary and
artistic claims are slender to excess.

In the *Hundred Merry Tales*, 1526,
there is the story of the lad who took
his shoes to be mended, whence comes
the information to us that the charge
for this kind of work was at that period
threepence. Then, in another item of
the series, which in its totality is decidedly unconventional, we perceive how
young fellows just emerging from boy-
hood wore the hair on the upper lip as
well as the beard. The story *Of the
Courtier and the Carter* aptly serves to
throw light on a point which does not
appear to be sufficiently understood—
the application of the terms *cart* and
carter to ordinary vehicles for the conveyance of travellers of all degrees,—so
much so that the rough, old-fashioned

lawyer, desirous of an audience with Queen Elizabeth, while she was on a journey, cried out to her coachman, "Stop thy cart, good fellow, stop thy cart!" and the ancient French hunting chariots were merely an evolution from the primitive agricultural model.

It is difficult to resist the temptation to smile at the whimsical suggestion of the curate "who preached the articles of the Creed," that such as were not satisfied about them from his communication had better go to Coventry and see them on the stage at the Corpus Christi play. What a vivid glimpse rises before us of the feeling and costume of three or four centuries ago, when we read the account given in another of the *Tales*, "of the man that desired to be set on the pillory," in order that, while he was there, his confederates in the crowd might pick the honest folks' pockets and empty the butchers' aprons, as they gaped at the spectacle!

The expedients for swindling which formerly throve, enter not a little into these miscellanies; and the drollery of

the incidents of a fraud naturally outlive
the temporary elements. The narrative
of a sharper, who is, by the way, described as "a merry man," and who
distributed bills announcing the performance of a play, belongs to the earlier
years of Elizabeth; but it was a trick
repeated, doubtless, more than once.
The particular story is laid somewhere
about 1567, and it establishes several
curious details respecting the theatrical
exhibitions of that date. The scene
was Northumberland Place, in the city
of London, and the proceedings were to
commence at two in the afternoon. Two
men were stationed at the gate with a
box to take the money—a penny or a
halfpenny at least—and as soon as the
fellow conceived that there was no likelihood of collecting more, he sent the
two box-keepers in to "keep the room,"
mounted a horse which waited for him
at an adjoining inn, and rode off to
Barnet.

This episode is additionally curious
and interesting, because it anticipates
by almost forty years a precisely similar

adventure placed on record by Chamberlain the letter-writer as having occurred within his knowledge in 1602. In both cases the actors were advertised to be *amateurs*, which, as the piece was to be presented on a scaffold in the marketplace, was a novel attraction and a happy stroke.

The epigram of Sir Thomas More on one who took the fly out of a glass of water, and replaced it when he had done drinking, has been made the basis for a jest; but was itself founded on the common superstition that such an act was lucky.

The current pronunciation of an early West of England name underlies the pleasantry that Master You having wedded Mistress You, he was ever afterwards known as Master W. The old Devonshire Yeos were probably called *Yous* by their provincial neighbours.

There is an abundance of historical sayings with a facetious vein or tag; and some of them are highly interesting little traits and sidelights. During the Wars of the Roses, an unfortunate man met in succession with two parties, of whom one was for Edward IV. and the other for Henry VI. To the inquiry of the first he replied that he was Henry's man, wherefore they beat him; and to the second that he was Edward's, which brought him the same luck. So the next time, to be quite safe, he declared himself to be the Devil's man; and when they said, "Then the Devil go with thee!" "Amen!" quoth he: "he is the best master I've served to-day."

There are two survivals about a priest just at the epoch of the Reformation; they are evidently little touches from life. This learned clerk is made to preach a sermon on Charity, and in it to avouch that no man can get to heaven without charity, except only the King's Grace, God save him! Then, when the royal visitors came down to his parts to make their report, he was interrogated as to what he did and how he passed his time. "I occupy myself in reading the New Testament," says he. "That is very well," say the Commissioners; "but prythee, Sir, who made the New Testament?" "That did King

Henry the Eighth," replies the priest,
" Lord have mercy on his soul ! "

There is a strong air of verisimilitude
in the salutation of Richard III., as he
was collecting his forces in Thicket's
field, by the Northern man : " Diccon,
Diccon, by the mis, I'se blith that
thaust king"; and there are in the same
tract (*Merry Tales and Quick Answers*) a
couple of characteristic scraps, the only
remaining footprints, as it were, of the
Canon of Hereford, whose deficiency in
intelligence and scholarship they celebrate.

Gossip and satire concerning the priesthood seem, from a very remote period,
to have been received with relish and
tolerance ; but tales exposing the rapa-
city, ignorance and licentiousness of
the cloth were circulated from political
motives with even greater eagerness and
immunity just prior to that grand climax
which abrogated the papal supremacy in
England for ever.

It is necessary, and not difficult, to
distinguish between narrated incidents,
which veritably belong to a specific
vicinity, and such fictitious variants as

are merely localised for the nonce. Of
the latter the jest-books, which contributed so largely to the activity of the
press from the accession of the Stuarts
to their restoration, are rich in examples,
as I have already pointed out. *Pasquil's
Jests* is one of the worst offenders in
this way. "How a merchant lost his
purse between Waltham and London"
is nothing more than a new-birth of the
account in *Merry Tales and Quick
Answers*, where Ware is the place
specified; and "How mad Coomes of
Stapforth, when his wife was drowned,
sought her against the stream," reproduces
No. 55 of the same older miscellany,
which is itself copied and varied from
a Latin *fabliau*. Manchester, Hertford-
shire, Kingston, Lincolnshire, and other
neighbourhoods are fixed as the theatres
of adventures in these books, without
the slightest eye to topographical fitness.
The anterior publications had perhaps set
the fashion to some extent, and notably
so the Gothamite Tales; but the resuscita-
tion of used matter with some superficial
investiture of novelty became a sort of

necessity, when the popular demand for these wares increased out of proportion to the supply.

In certain of the collections, on the contrary, and most especially and largely in the two Tudor ones so often quoted, we meet with little dramatic scenes, laid here or there, with a fair accompaniment of probability in support of the attribution. I shall take the course of referring those who may care to follow this part of the argument to the *Hundred Merry Tales,*—

No. 29. Of the Welshman, who said that he could get but a little mail.

No. 33. Of the priest, who said Our Lady was not so curious a woman.

No. 40. Of Master Skelton, who brought the Bishop of Norwich two pheasants.

No. 71. Of the priest that would say two gospels for a groat.

No. 87. Of Master Whittington's dream.

And to *Merry Tales and Quick Answers,*—

No. 54. Of Master Vavasor and Turpin his man.

No. 94. Of the Cheshire man called Evelyn.

No. 132. Of him that sold two loads of hay.

No. 134. How the image of the Devil was lost and sought.

I think that all the articles which I have just indicated manifest a realism of portraiture and complexion which should commend and endear them to the studiers and lovers of the old English life ; in the edition of the *Hundred Merry Tales* which the Royal Library at Göttingen owns, and which I have lately reprinted in facsimile, there is a further item falling within the same category—the highly amusing and doubtless veracious tale of the Maltman of Colebrook, which may be appropriately bracketed with the one " of him that sold two loads of hay."

Both are, in fact, relations of actual events thrown into a readable shape with a modicum of colouring.

14

CHAPTER XX.

ESIDES these two repertories,
the *Merry Tales of Skelton*
contain a racy and diverting
account of a trick played by the
poet on a Kendal man, with whom
he was riding from Oxford to London.
They baited at Uxbridge, and while his
companion was out of the room, Skelton
took his cap, which he had left behind
on the table, inserted some butter inside
the lining, and put it back in its place.
When the owner returned, he placed it
on his head, of which the warmth soon
had the anticipated effect.   The butter

ran down the fellow's face and neck, and Skelton assured him that he had the sweating sickness. The Kendal man was in great terror of his life, and Skelton advised him to go to bed at once. A little hot water applied to the cap and its proprietor set matters right ; the joke was explained and forgiven, and the two rode on to town the next morning. Such practical hoaxes were doubtless frequent enough ; and the laureated parson of Diss was never, one is apt to apprehend, so thoroughly at home as when he had something of the kind in hand.

The modern works offer in a similar manner, and perhaps, on the whole, to a greater extent, authentic examples of local occurrences. There is the celebrated adventure of Sir Thomas More with the lunatic on the flat roof of his house at Chelsea, which runs somewhat parallel to one which the Duke of Wellington had with a crazy fellow at Apsley House :—

" When Sir Thomas More was one day on the flat-leaded roof of his house at Chelsea, a lunatic succeeded somehow in getting to him, and tried to throw him down, crying, 'Leap, Tom, leap!' The Chancellor was in his dressing-gown, and, besides, was too old a man to have any chance against the madman. Sir Thomas had a little dog with him. 'Let's throw him down first,' said he, 'and see what good fun that will be'; so the fellow took up the animal, and threw him down. 'Now,' said More, 'run and fetch him back, and let us try again, for I think it is good sport. The madman went, and as soon as he had disappeared, More rose and secured the door."

As representatives of the same class, belonging to different periods, the subjoined must serve :—

"A gentleman, who possessed a small estate in Gloucestershire, was allured to town by the promises of the Duke of Newcastle, who, for many months, kept him in constant attendance, until, the poor man's patience being quite exhausted, he one morning called upon his patron, and told him that he had at length got a place. The Duke very cordially shook him by the hand, and congratulated him on his good fortune, telling him that in a few days a good thing would have been in his gift; 'but pray, sir,' added he, 'where is your place?' 'In the Gloucester coach,' replied he: 'I secured it last night.'"

"Pennant, the antiquary, had an unaccountable antipathy to wigs. Dining at Chester with

an officer who wore this covering for the head,
when they had drunk pretty freely, after many
wistful looks, Pennant started up, seized the
caxon, and threw it into the fire. The wig was
in a moment in flames, and so was the officer,
who immediately drew his sword. Downstairs
flies Pennant, and the officer after him, through
all the streets of Chester ; but the former escaped
through superior local knowledge."

" A quack-doctor, haranguing the populace at
Hammersmith, said, 'To this village I owe my
birth and education ; I dearly love it and its inhabitants, and will cheerfully give a present of
a crown to every one who will accept it.' The
audience received this notice with infinite satisfaction. 'Here, ladies and gentlemen,' added
he, putting his hand into a bag, and taking out
a parcel of packets, 'these inestimable medicines
I usually sell for five and sixpence each, but in
favour of this, my native village, I will take
sixpence apiece.'"

Where the profusion of illustrative
matter is inexhaustible, a survey of a
subject is bound to limit itself to suggestion and sample. But the remarks and
indications which have been afforded,
must testify at any rate to the residence
in these vast stores, on which I have
been drawing, of a utility and dignity in

numerous cases beyond their value as
mere temporary vehicles for distraction
and mirth, and to their claim to a subsidiary place among historical and social
monuments.

The localisation of interest in an adventure or incident does not seem at first to
have struck those who laboured for the
public entertainment as a commercial ex-
pedient deserving of study and trial.   But
as the volume of jocular and anecdotal
literature swelled, and the competition
for favour and novelty grew keener in
proportion, the resort to new devices for
imparting a relish and edge to old properties comprised the association of jests
which had weathered numberless seasons,
with some fresh person or neighbourhood.
Hence arises the multitude of collections
and headings identifying books of the
present class or portions of their contents
with particular places and particular individuals, such as the *Cobbler of Canterbury*,
the Footpost of Dover, and the *Gravesend
Tilt-Boat*, or, in the case of personality,
the numerous entries in *Pasquil's Jests* of
stories of Merry Andrew of Manchester,

Coomes of Stapforth, and so on, all of
which are resuscitations of stale and bygone material.

The work which led the way and set
the mode in this direction was perhaps
*The Merry Tales of the Mad Men of
Gotham*, by Andrew Borde. It was a
dexterous and attractive method of sub-
stituting for the vague generalisations of
anterior compilers "a local habitation and
a name." It fixed the geography of the
event, and established its authenticity
beyond dispute ; for, as the phrase is in
the narratives of early murders and other
phenomena, any gentleman, who doubted
the veracity of the writer, might go and
inquire for himself on the spot.

The idea of lending a local colouring
and flavour to anecdotes originated, however, probably among the early Italian
collectors of *burle* and *facetie*, of which
some are transferred to our own miscellanies; and the practice dates back to a
period when the literary life was bounded
by the walls of capitals, or did not at
most overstep their outskirts.

The stories, which present themselves

in this class of book about the inhabitants
of Scotland and Wales, generally bear
on the pilfering propensities occasioned
by poverty, facilitated by geographical
position, and justified by the sense of
wrong.   Their habits of parsimony were
acquired by the Scots during centuries
of miserable and oppressive misgovern-
ment, and survived the stern necessity
out of which they arose.   The Welsh
borderer, if one judges from the tales
current about him in the old *facetiæ*,
and from what history itself reveals, combined with an addiction to " lifting " and
drunkenness a certain pusillanimity of
spirit, which may be less injurious to the
community, but is more to be contemned
in the individual.   He was too often,
besides being a thief and a sot, a sneaking
rascal.   The nursery rhyme about Taffy
is a piece of veracious tradition, an accurate reflex of the state of society in the
lower grades in the Principality down to
the last century, or even until Wales was
brought within the operation of more
stringent laws and a more efficient police.
The humorous side of the numberless

legendary anecdotes about the Cambro-
Britons has been rendered abundantly
visible by the gatherers of *Ana* ; but
when we regard this material in the
aggregate, and explore a little beneath
the surface, we arrive at the interesting
discovery that: in this, as in every other
group of similar relics, there is a good
deal deserving of careful study and colla-
tion, and that the whole body of such
literature ought henceforth to be, much
more than it has, I think, hitherto been,
treated as a branch of the national
Folk-lore.

The merriments at the expense of Taffy,
if they do not turn on his dishonesty,
are pretty sure to deal with his passion
for liquor and toasted cheese. Congruity
and fitness are seldom respected in this
line of literary work; and in one of the
Hundred Merry Tales, St. Peter, upon
the representation of God that the Welsh-
men in heaven, with their noisy ways,
were a nuisance to all the rest, engages
to get rid of them. He goes to the
entrance-gates and shouts *Cause bobe!*
and forthwith every Cambro-Briton rushes

out to see where his favourite delicacy
is to be had.   The sly apostle, the
moment they are all outside, closes the
door, and the Christian Elysium is its old
self again.

This whimsical piece of invention may
be bracketed with a second narrated in
the so-called *Tales of Skelton,* in which
the other gastronomic failing of the Principality is amiably depicted ; although the
two stories are of different types, the one
being a pleasant extravagance, while the
other, which I now give, may have been
an actual incident.

It professes to be an account " how
the Welshman did desire Skelton to aid
him in his suit to the king for a patent
to sell drink."

"Skelton, when he was in London, went to
the King's Court, where there did come to him
a Welshman, saying, 'Sir, it is so, that many
do come up out of my country to the King's
Court, and some get of the King by patent a
castle, and some a park, and some a forest, and
some one fee and some another, and they live
like honest men ; and I should live as honestly
as the best, if I might have a patent for selling
good drink.   Wherefore I pray you write a

petition for me to give into the King's hands.
'Very good,' said Skelton. 'Sit down,' said the
Welshman, 'and write, then.' 'What shall I
write?' asked Skelton. The Welshman said,
'Write *Drink*. Now write *More drink*.' 'What
now?' said Skelton. 'Write now *A great deal
of drink;* and put to all this drink *A little crumb
of bread, and a great deal of drink to it,* and read
out what you have written.' '*Drink, more drink,
and a great deal of drink, and a little crumb of
bread, and a great deal of drink to it.*' Then quoth
the Welshman, 'put out *the little crumb of bread*,
and set down *all drink and no bread ;* and if I
might have this petition signed by the King, I
care for no more, as long as I live.' 'Well, then,'
said Skelton, 'when you have got yours passed,
I will try to get another for bread, that you with
your drink, and I with my bread, may seek our
living together with bag and staff.'"

Whether Andrew Borde, the pleasant
Sussex Doctor of Physic, really wrote
the little book of stories about Skelton,
whom he might very well have personally
known, must be numbered among the
uncertainties ; but Borde's estimate of
Taffy is cognate to that of Skelton himself, as delivered to us in the book and
in the *Hundred Merry Tales*. For in
his *Introduction of Knowledge*, 1542, the

Doctor puts into the mouth of his
Cambro-Briton these lines :—

"I am a Welshman, and do dwell in Wales;
 I have loved to search budgets, and look in
     mails,"

which seems to portray the predatory
borderer and the thief by breeding and
instinct.

It is perhaps, at ·the same time, a
matter for speculation whether these
traits of Welsh character were not more
current after the accession of the Tudors.
Henry the Seventh, as his *Privy Purse
Expenses* establish, was very lavish in his
presents to his countrymen; and the
royal partiality tended very possibly to
render them unpopular in England, and
to bring their foibles and frailties into
print. The very tale above given reads
like a burlesque on the importunity of
Taffy for privileges and monopolies at
Henry's hands, and at the same time
jeers pretty broadly at his propensity for
intemperance.

There is a story of a Scottish minister
who went South, and was invited to stay

to dinner at an acquaintance's. After
they had dined, the whiskey was brought
in; the minister took to it kindly, and
accepted a proposal to remain till the
morning. As the spare bed had to be
aired, and there was not time to prepare
the warming-pan, the lady of the house
told Jenny the maidservant to undress,
and get into the bed to warm the sheets
for their guest; but Jenny unluckily (or
otherwise) fell asleep, and when the
visitor went up, he found her still in
possession. "Well," said he to himself,
"the dinner was good; the whiskey was
capital; but—this is hospitality indeed!"

We will not pursue the narration
further. It is obviously a parody on the
conventional order of things, having by
possibility some indebtedness to the
simple manners of a bygone time and
less fastidious sleeping arrangements. The
improvised warming-pan might have
suggested itself to the guidwife; but we
cherish a suspicion that the *ex-post-facto*
improver is answerable for the pleasantry
as it stands. In jocular history everybody is at angles to real life; people do

precisely what they ought not to do, say
what they ought not to say, are found
where they ought not to be found.
That is the soul of the matter; and
therein lies the cunning of the wire-
puller. He is for general purposes what
Grobianus is for Cato and Mrs. Grundy.
He seldom invents; he has a preference
for ready-made material which he can
employ as a groundwork or starting-
point; for a familiar name goes a long
way. The artist has to be wary how
he deals with his puppet or lay-figure;
he treads upon eggs a little; much
depends on the turn given; the anecdote which he tells need not be true,
God knows; it may be naughty within
bounds; but it must be amusing. That
is peremptory.

The *Bull*, in its jocular acceptation,
has been commonly viewed as a genuine
Irish product; but may it not be, on
the contrary, of Italian and ecclesiastical
descent? The papal brief, in the first
place, borrowed its name from the leaden
seal which was attached to it; the odium
under which Popery and its supporters

fell in the time of Elizabeth next led to
the passage of the *bull* into our voca-
bulary as a term of ridicule or contempt;
and, finally, when the strong political
feeling had subsided, the expression stood
for any piece of harmless extravagance
or hyperbolical bravado. These side-
growths of meaning are curious and
instructive enough, and present many
strange and unsuspected survivals. To
go no farther than the word before us,
the modern Italian attaches to his letter
a *bolla* without reflecting on its actual
and archaic significance, just as he per-
petuates bygone methods of locomotion
by continuing to call the railway carriage
a *poste*.

Perhaps the characterisation of an
imperial German decree of 1356 as "*a
golden bull*" is not more alien to the
original sense and function of the word
than its pressure into service by the
Italian of our day to signify a postage-
stamp.

INDEX.